"I found *Last Words* by Rob Nash to be full of gospel encouragement. When the world is so full of distractions to the soul and spiritual life, it is refreshing to read and think about what God accomplished on behalf of his people through the death of his Son, Jesus Christ. *Last Words* makes a great devotional tool as it provides reasons to give thanks and praise to God on almost every page."

Norm Wakefield, President of Elijah Ministries

"Pastor Rob Nash offers helpful insights into the background and context of Jesus's final words. *Last Words* is a spiritually refreshing treatise for anyone who desires to reflect more deeply on Christ's experience on the cross."

Brian Weber, Executive Minister of Converge MidAtlantic

"Other than the Bible itself, *Last Words* is the most insightful, interesting, compelling, and profound book I've ever read about the cross. As I pondered this in-depth exploration of the last statements of Christ, my mind was challenged, my heart was warmed, and my faith was strengthened. Rob Nash has written a biblically precise masterpiece—one that not only brings forth a more thoughtful, thorough understanding of the redemptive work of Jesus, but also encourages God's pattern for Christian living."

Ginger Hubbard, Best-selling author of *Don't Make Me Count to Three* and *I Can't Believe You Just Said That!*

"I find *Last Words* an excellent resource for every serious student of Scripture desiring to wrestle with the last words of our Savior. The book is filled with rich truths, deep meditations, and strong practical applications. Be prepared to think deeply and be stretched personally."

Gary Rohrmayer, President of Converge MidAmerica

"Rob Nash explains that the brief and sometimes cryptic final words of our Lord on the cross unpack profound realities in heaven and on earth. This warm devotional work will take you beyond the surface to explore the depths of the gospel. As you read it, your passion for God will be inflamed, your gratitude deepened, and your worship of our great God and Savior enriched, all to the glory of God."

Craig Parro, President of Leadership Resources

"This book reads with the immediacy and richness of a film. The seven phrases Jesus gasps out on the cross serve as touch points for Nash to explore layered flashbacks to Old Testament rituals, Hebrew prophecies, and the Gospel stories. But the real beauty of Nash's method is this: he personalizes each phrase right down into the nitty-gritty of the reader's present life. While this book is short enough to read in a single sitting as I did, it is full enough to provide seven weekly meditative chapters leading up to Easter, which is how I intend to read it next!"

J. A. Myhre, Author of The Rwendigo Tales series; physician serving with Serge in East Africa

"We are fascinated by the last words a person speaks. We ponder them, even dissect them, looking for meaning. Since the church's earliest days, Christians have pondered the last words the greatest Man ever spoke as a mortal. Here Rob Nash joins this ancient succession of meditation, dissecting the dying words of the divine Son. And he shows us that in them is a world of profoundly personal meaning, for Jesus meant them for each of us."

Jon Bloom, Author; board chair and cofounder of Desiring God Ministries

"Robert J. Nash's exposition of the last words of Jesus is faithfully and vividly presented, drawing from the other passages of Scripture in order to show their theological implications. These gospel-saturated truths are then helpfully applied to the reader, who is encouraged not only to apply the truth personally but also to share it with others. I heartily recommend this book."

Jim Newheiser, Director of the Christian Counseling Program and Associate Professor of Practical Theology at Reformed Theological Seminary, Charlotte, NC

"I truly enjoyed this fresh look into the last words of Jesus. When you study them deeply, you will see what the Roman soldier who stood at the foot of the cross saw: surely, Jesus is the Son of God! In these last words of Jesus, we see that hanging on the cross was not just a good man, but the God-man who died to pay the price that God demands for the sin and rebellion of humanity. This book is not just for Easter; it is for everyone to read and reread year-round to have your heart and your mind grounded in the awe of the cross. You will never partake of the Lord's Table the same way again."

Steve Leston, President of To Every Tribe

Last Words

Seven Sayings
from the Heart of Christ
on the Cross

Robert J. Nash

New
Growth
Press

newgrowthpress.com

New Growth Press, Greensboro, NC 27404
www.newgrowthpress.com

Cover Design: Faceout Books, faceoutstudio.com
Interior Typesetting and eBook: LParnell Book Services

ISBN 978-1-64507-040-5 (Print)
ISBN 978-1-64507-041-2 (eBook)

Library of Congress Cataloging-in-Publication Data

Names: Nash, Robert J., 1977– author.
Title: Last words : seven sayings from the heart of Christ on the cross /
    Robert J. Nash.
Description: Greensboro, NC : New Growth Press, [2020] | Includes
    bibliographical references and index. | Summary: "Christ's final words
    on earth are full of forgiveness, hope, and compassion. *Last Words* by
    Robert J. Nash explores a fresh perspective on the obedience of the
    cross, revealing the heart of God who sent his son to die. Find new
    meaning in the power and hope of his death"— Provided by publisher.
Identifiers: LCCN 2019034704 (print) | LCCN 2019034705 (ebook) | ISBN
    9781645070405 (trade paperback) | ISBN 9781645070412 (ebook)
Subjects: LCSH: Jesus Christ—Seven last words.
Classification: LCC BT457 .N37 2020 (print) | LCC BT457 (ebook) | DDC
    232.96/35—dc23
LC record available at https://lccn.loc.gov/2019034704
LC ebook record available at https://lccn.loc.gov/2019034705

Printed in the United States of America

28 27 26 25 24 23 22 21 20   1 2 3 4 5

Contents

DEDICATED

TO MY LORD AND SAVIOR JESUS CHRIST.

He is my greatest treasure, only hope,
and the one whom I trust.
May you get glory through these words.

Foreword

⟳

The final words of our Lord are brief and sometimes cryptic, perhaps not surprising given, as Rob Nash explains, the suffocating cruelty of the cross. Yet he also explains that these simple words unpack profound realities in heaven and on earth.

Rob helps us grasp a far fuller understanding of the seven last words of Jesus. Like a wise guide, he takes us back into the Old Testament Scriptures which inform these last words. Rob also reintroduces us to the characters who experienced the horrors of that first Good Friday—the co-crucified thief; the sneering religious leaders; Mary, the grieving mother of Jesus; and the centurion who was perhaps the first to understand what it all meant.

This warm devotional work will take you beyond the surface to explore the depths of the gospel. As you read it, your passion for God will be inflamed, your gratitude deepened, and your worship of our great God and Savior enriched, all to the glory of God.

Craig Parro, President of Leadership Resources

Acknowledgments

⮾

I want to thank several people who helped me put this work together. Bob and Judy, Lori, Kari, Chris, Judy, Rick, David, Emily, Sara, and Dave and Sue, thank you all so much. Speaking in public is different than writing. Your honest counsel has helped make this what it is. I want to thank Sawyer Highlands Church and Pastor Jeff Dryden. They have given me the freedom to shape our Good Fridays around my creative exploration of the last words of Christ. I also want to thank New Growth Press for helping me make this labor of my soul as something everyone can enjoy for years to come. Specifically, I want to thank Tom, Mollie, Audra, and the rest of the New Growth staff for their hard work. In addition, I want to thank Ruth Castle, Cheryl White, Jack Klumpenhower, and Barbara Juliani for their editing eyes. Finally, I want to thank my wife who puts up with the late nights and early morning antics that led to the completion of this project. She is my best friend and a magnificent avenue of God's grace to me.

Introduction

❧

The last words of a hero or heroine in a story pack a punch. The final chapter of a book ties up loose ends. Epitaphs and eulogies have a summarizing power. Phone calls, visits, and whispers of those on hospice become riches locked away in the fading memories of those left behind. Jesus shared seven last thoughts as he died that contain a wealth of meaning we should not forget or neglect. This book seeks to mine those words to challenge the soul.

The idea for this book began on a cold spring in 2003. Newly married, I was living in Minneapolis, studying at Bethel Seminary in St. Paul. It was Friday night. My wife and I drove from our apartment on campus to church. That evening I experienced one of the most powerful messages I have ever heard. The words of the homily blended darkness, passion, and melody to the pain of the day Jesus died. The stone church's sanctuary was dimly lit, the music set to a minor key, and the majority of us wore somber colors of black. At the end of the service, we were asked to exit quietly. Year after year, the pastor shared that same message with similar effect. Each time it struck a chord in the heart. In the following decade, I began to wonder if I could explore more of the meaning behind Jesus's last words. I believe Jesus's final words have a larger message that the church needs to hear today.

I am a happy optimist. Life is comfortable with fresh starts and cups half full. Each morning is filled with beauty, blessings, coffee, and new beginnings. I am amazed at the sunrise, the fresh breeze, the dew drops, the song of the cardinal, the blue skies, the crashing waves, and the rest of God's creation. However, as a pastor, counselor, elder, and chaplain over the years, I have seen the harsher side of life. I have met death in the emergency room. I have walked into divorce court. I have heard stories of abuse, listened to heartache and suffering that rips one's heart out and uses up all of one's tears. My role has given me a passport into a world that is unkind and often downright evil. It seems that everyone has hurt and pain, even optimists. Jesus's last words meet us in those moments. His scant words connect our longing for forgiveness, need to be loved, yearning for someone to understand, and offer us hope and so much more.

What does God's Word say to those who are stuck, bound up, or wounded? God speaks to those in agony at the cross. He understands. He endured death. Good Friday, the day Jesus died, takes us on a journey of despair, desolation, and transports us to a place of comfort, and consolation. Meditating on his last words helps us, puts difficulties in perspective, sin in its place, and opens our eyes to the expanse of God's affection for us.

Here are Jesus's seven last statements made while on the cross:

- "Father, forgive them, for they know not what they do" (Luke 23:34).
- "Truly, I say to you, today you will be with me in paradise" (Luke 23:43).

- "Woman, behold, your son!" Then he said to the disciple, "Behold, your mother!" (John 19:26–27).
- "My God, my God, why have you forsaken me?" (Matthew 27:46).
- "I thirst" (John 19:28).
- "It is finished" (John 19:30).
- "Father, into your hands I commit my spirit!" (Luke 23:46).

These last words dynamically teach who Jesus is, what he was about, and why he came. They offer solace and instruction for all who will listen. Will you listen? Explore them with me as you read and reflect on your own spiritual journey.

1

Forgive

"Father, forgive them,
for they know not what they do." (Luke 23:34)

⁓

What we see today as a beautiful cross, an expression of religious art set in precious metals or stained glass, was a sign in Jesus's day of wickedness, punishment, and judgment. The cross meant humiliation and prolonged suffering, torture, and shame.

Jesus carried the massive top beam, weighing about a hundred pounds, on his shoulders as he marched to his death. Sleepless, beaten, and frail, he fell under its weight. Soldiers seized a nearby man, Simon of Cyrene, who was likely in town for Passover. They forced him to help a different Passover sacrifice, Jesus, carry his beam up a hill of death.

Jesus, the Nazarene, went to Golgotha, the place of the skull. Naked, he was laid down on the wood. Large nails, like railroad spikes, were pressed against his skin. A soldier raised a hammer. Blow fell again, and again, one after another, rupturing wrists and feet, exploding nerves, binding Jesus in place. Can you imagine how that felt?

When you died on a cross, it was not from bleeding to death. Death on a cross came slowly, from asphyxiation. Every time a crucified person took a breath, he would have to lift himself up by the nails pressing down on wounds, stressing bones and tendons and ligaments. Nerves would detonate with pain. Air would fill lungs and then, in exhaustion, the crucified would fall back on those same nails holding him up. Up and down, up and down they went. This could go on for days. To speed up the process, soldiers would break the legs of the crucified so they could not get any more air to breathe. So Good Friday went: Jesus gasping for air, pain in the wounds, gasping for air, and pain in the wounds, on and on and on and on, until he saw his final breath. Exhausted, abused, hungry, and choking, he gave up his life.

Why? Why would the Son of God suffer excruciating misery? I think we can answer that question best by exploring each phrase he uttered. The first thing he said on the cross was a prayer for the Father to forgive the very people who were killing him. Why? The injustice, the atrocity, the insanity of that pivotal moment in history—yet, he spoke a word of clemency? His breath did not come cheaply. He choked those words out. Why would he spend a breath asking his Father to forgive, of all people, those executioners?

JESUS AND FORGIVENESS

To answer that question, let us look at what Jesus had earlier said about forgiveness. In his ministry, he talked about it dozens of times. I think he did so because people carry loads of guilt, shame, bitterness, and hurt. People regret things from decades past and often run from it all. People need forgiveness.

At the same time, people hold onto grudges. They shut down paths of peace, and embrace generational feuds. Some avoid church because of guilt, while others switch churches because they would rather start over than forgive. People make jokes, tell lies, and brainwash themselves into thinking they are fine, or events never happened or if they did, they are not that big of a deal. However, people don't really move on, they just bury their problems. As a pastor, I see it and hear this regularly. People come up with do-it-yourself solutions to their hurt and sin, and miss God's remedy.

Jesus confronts our attempts to fix ourselves and presents the only path of peace. We see the first hint of this in Jesus's teaching at the Sermon on the Mount. He taught that our attitude toward other people indicates our understanding of God's forgiveness. He said, "For if you forgive others their trespasses, your heavenly Father will also forgive you, but if you do not forgive others their trespasses, neither will your Father forgive your trespasses" (Matthew 6:14–15). Not only do we need forgiveness, we need to learn to offer it.

This can seem impossible. However, Jesus says more is at stake than we may know when we refuse to forgive. God's forgiveness is connected to ours. Jesus taught that God will hold us to the standard we hold others. He wants us to be merciful, kind, and forgiving as God is. He wants us to let go of bitterness, anger, and grudges. How?

Forgiveness does not come easy or naturally. How can we forgive as we have been forgiven? In the abstract, Jesus's teaching seems simple. It is easy to be forgiving if it is merely words. However, how do we forgive when we have been blindsided by injustice? Think about real wrongs done to you. How do you obey Jesus in light of those? How do we comply with Jesus's teaching or even come close to his example? We know how important forgiveness is, but when we are swimming in pain, this call to forgive can seem insurmountable.

Happily, Jesus's teaching on and his example of forgiveness did not end with a sermon. As we explore further, he explains how we can love our enemies to the point of even offering them forgiveness.

Peter, the disciple, heard Jesus's teaching, and it confused him. He asked Jesus how often a person should forgive. Maybe there is a limit, or a point where people just exhaust forgiveness? To Peter's chagrin, Jesus basically answered that if a person repents (turns away from his or her sin), forgive him every time. Literally, he said "seventy times seven." That was more than a three-strikes-and-you're-out policy. In a parallel account Jesus says if the offender sins and repents seven times in a single day, forgive every time (Luke 17:4).

Every time? How in the world can we offer forgiveness to what looks like a half-hearted apology? Are we really going to think they mean what they say after the third time? They probably are going to just sin again, don't you think?

Jesus responds to this question about forgiveness with a wonderful story. He tells a tale of a servant who had an astronomical debt. The servant came to his king and asked for relief. What did the king do? He released him of his obligation. Simple and astounding, that huge debt was forgiven. Not too long afterward, that same servant ran into a man who owed him a comparable pittance. The man could not pay. Furious, the servant had his debtor thrown into prison. News traveled fast. The king heard about this turn of events and called the servant back.

Hear what words Jesus has the king speak:

> "You wicked servant! I forgave you all that debt because you pleaded with me. And should not you have had mercy on your fellow servant, as I had mercy on you?" And in anger his master delivered him to the jailers, until he should pay all his debt. So also my heavenly Father will do to every one of you, if you do not forgive your brother from your heart." (Matthew 18:32–35)

The point is clear: we must understand the spiritual debt God has forgiven us. This should aid us in forgiving the debt others owe us. That is how we can obey Jesus's teaching. Understanding the sin originally forgiven us gives us the power to extend mercy to those who wrong us and make a poor attempt to get right. If we have been forgiven a million dollars in debt, then remembering whose turn it is to pay for lunch is not as important. The key is perspective.

Jesus beautifully illustrated the importance of this perspective again at the home of a Pharisee named Simon. Everyone was eating and having a grand old time. A woman of the city entered. She took some expensive perfume and started anointing Jesus and wiping his feet with her hair and tears. The host was beside himself. She had barged into his home and threw herself on his guest. This woman was presumably known for her loose living, hence Simon's revulsion. Add to that, the grassroots religious superstar didn't show any reservation with this over-the-top affection. Addressing Simon's thoughts with a lesson, Jesus said:

> "A certain moneylender had two debtors. One owed five hundred denarii, and the other fifty. When they could not pay, he cancelled the debt of both. Now which of them will love him more?" Simon answered, "The one, I suppose, for whom he cancelled the larger debt." And he said to him, "You have judged rightly." Then turning toward the woman he said to Simon, "Do you see this woman? I entered your house; you gave me no water for my feet, but she has wet my feet with her tears and wiped them with her hair. You gave me no kiss, but from the time I came in she has not ceased to kiss my feet. You did not anoint my head with oil, but she has anointed my feet with ointment. Therefore I tell you, her sins, which are many, are forgiven—for she loved much. But he who

is forgiven little, loves little." And he said to her, "Your sins are forgiven." (Luke 7:41–48)

He who is forgiven little, loves little. Forgiveness was personal and specific in Jesus's day, as in ours. Jesus forgave this woman her sin against God. This audacious assertion and ability shocked the dinner party, but even more stunning was the key to forgiveness he taught here. We *can* become people of gratitude and love amidst our hurt and pain. Jesus says those who have a tangible understanding of their forgiven spiritual debt become more attuned to gratitude and love. That makes sense. The woman obviously is so much more appreciative of Jesus than Simon. The forgiven sinner has a better perspective of Jesus than the religious leader.

Have you experienced forgiveness from a friend or family member and seen how it healed the relationship? Have you been overwhelmed by God's love and forgiveness? Have you wept tears of appreciation and contrition? This woman had.

Maybe you find yourself relating to Simon. You don't feel like you have been that bad or need forgiveness. Maybe you find it easy to look down on others. Remember the story of the unmerciful servant. Paul taught in 2 Corinthians 5:14, "The love of Christ controls us." Some versions translate the word for control as "compels." The love of Christ compels us. The rocket fuel for forgiving others is a keen awareness of our own forgiven debt. How do we forgive when it is hard? We must move toward the perspective of the forgiven. We must see ourselves as we are.

JESUS AND SINNERS

All of us are debtors, even if we don't believe it. This can be hard to grasp in a culture that tends to avoid admission of guilt and ownership of sin. Sin is any thought, word, or deed that falls short of God's ideal. We sin in doing things we should not and in not doing things we should. We sin in big ways and little ways. We sin consciously and unconsciously. Our sins add up. Centuries before all this, the prophet Jeremiah commented on humanity's depravity. He wrote, "The heart is deceitful above all things, and desperately sick; who can understand it?" (Jeremiah 17:9). We all are debt holders in need of Christ's forgiveness.

We hear Jesus's heart for sinners like us in his words of grace and mercy on the cross. We owe him everything. Some might think that is not a big deal, but forgiveness does not come cheap. Forgiveness acknowledges sin and hurt and brokenness and pain. It does not ignore the hurt or pretend everything is back to how it used to be. Instead, it absorbs the hurt and the cost. Jesus did not forgive with mere words; he forgave *on the cross*.

Jesus pointed to this hours before, in an upper room Passover celebration with his disciples.

> Now as they were eating, Jesus took bread, and after blessing it broke it and gave it to the disciples, and said, "Take, eat; this is my body." And he took a cup, and when he had given thanks he gave it to them, saying, "Drink of it, all of you, for this is my blood of the covenant, which is poured out for many for the forgiveness of sins. I tell you I will not drink again of this fruit of the vine until that day when I drink it new with you in my Father's kingdom." (Matthew 26:26–30)

What purchased our forgiveness? Jesus's blood was poured out. He took the bread and cup and infused new meaning in them. Instead of remembering the Jewish tradition of lambs slain in Egypt (Exodus 12:1–28), Jesus said the bread and wine represented his body and blood. He was the lamb to be slain to take away the sin of the world once and for all. His body and blood were a new covenant, echoing the past and looking forward to the future. The cross was a fulfillment of a promise, God's promise to bless every nation and offer forgiveness for the many who would believe (Genesis 12:1-3; John 1:29; 3:16-17; Hebrews 9:22-28).

Forgiveness was infinitely expensive. Jesus gave his life. He embraced the cross out of love. He did that for you. It was the plan from the beginning of time. He knew it. His action resonated within his heart. His heart was one of compassion, not rancor or rage or revenge. We eavesdrop on his plea for forgiveness at the cross and hear his heart of mercy for his persecutors. He has a fierce love for wayward people. Justice and mercy collided in those moments.

Moses taught, "For the life of the flesh is in the blood, and I have given it for you on the altar to make atonement for your souls, for it is the blood that makes atonement by the life" (Leviticus 17:11; see also Hebrews 9:22). Jesus knew that principle. He offered up his life as an atoning sacrifice to wipe debts clean. He gave his blood for his people, for forgiveness, for you. He believed in mercy, and lived out what he believed. He thought not of hunger or loneliness or injustice or pain or complaints in that moment, but of you.

At his core was compassion for those who were his enemies. Luke records that, days before, "when he drew near and saw the city [Jerusalem], he wept over it" (Luke 19:41). He wept over the city that would soon demand his death. Why? It was because of his compassion for people who knew not the full horror of what they do. We see this all though the Bible: God shows mercy on Adam after his rebellion in the garden of Eden, promising future redemption in the curse on the serpent. God shows mercy on Noah, preserving him through the flood and promising never to flood the earth again. God shows mercy on Abraham, promising to bless all people through him. God shows mercy on David, promising a future king who would reign forever—and be crucified on a Friday during Passover week, just outside David's capital city. David writes in Psalm 103:8, "The LORD is merciful and gracious, slow to anger and abounding in steadfast love." And so Jesus prayed, "Forgive them for they know not what they do," reflecting that heart of mercy.

God's justice and forgiveness unite at the cross. He executed justice and applied forgiveness. Jesus's prayer showed this disposition to God's followers. His heart was like his Father's. Peter wrote, "The Lord is not slow to fulfill his promise as some count slowness, but is patient toward you, not wishing that any should perish, but that all should reach repentance" (2 Peter 3:9). As Jesus was murdered, he thought of you. He loved you. He cared for you. He knew you. He died for you. That was the first thing his lips uttered, but not the last.

RESULTS

By day's end, the Father would answer Jesus's prayer, and some would believe in Jesus. A thief would be among that number, and a centurion in charge who declared, "Truly this was the Son of God!" (Matthew 27:54).

Forgiveness became available through Jesus's blood shed for you.

Grab it.

Take it.

Hold it.

Embrace it.

Embrace forgiveness. It was meted out in mercy on a wooden beam two thousand years ago. The wrath of God was poured out on the Son, so it would not be poured out on you. Justice was satisfied. Jesus chose it. He went to the cross willingly. Good Friday was good because it means your sins, condemnation, guilt, and shame were obliterated if you trust him. God forgives it all: pride, jealousy, envy, idolatry, laziness, lies, gossip, slander, suspicion, hatred, theft, fraud, abortion, addictions, violence, pornography, adultery, immorality, and perversion—by faith in Jesus's death. You do not have to live under the bondage of the past, or the fear of being found out. You are not shackled to old skeletons, dark deeds, or nagging regrets. Jesus suffered and died for it all and offers you mercy. He died to forgive.

REFLECTION

Reflect now on those first words of Christ on the cross. Take a moment to think through each step below:

See Your Need. What sins have you committed, or keep committing, that you fear Jesus won't forgive? Why do you think he won't forgive you?

See Jesus. Think about how far Jesus went to forgive even his executioners. Which aspects of Jesus's death on the cross most encourage you to come to him for forgiveness?

Go to God. When was the last time you asked God to forgive you for something? Describe that experience. What sin can you confess to God right now and enjoy forgiveness anew? What can you say to thank him for sending his Son to suffer and die in your place?

Go to Others. What grudges, bitterness, or shame comes between you and others? What makes it hard for you to forgive? What part of Jesus's teaching about the woman who anointed his feet might encourage you that you *can* have enough love to forgive? How might you move toward forgiveness of a person who has wronged you in the coming days?

Pray.

God, help me to know your grace and forgiveness
today as I think about who you are and what you
have done. Thank you for giving up your life for
mine. Thank you for suffering betrayals, insults,
false accusations, abuse, and death for my sin.
Bring to mind my wrongs, my sin, and my rebellion that made the cross necessary for me to be
right with you. Help me to grasp your mercy and
forgiveness demonstrated on the cross. Help me to
see your heart of mercy specifically for me. Help me
to offer that kind of forgiveness to others. Help me
to love my enemies as you loved me. Thank you for
Good Friday and your last words of forgiveness and
love.

2

Today

*"Truly, I say to you, today you will be with me
in paradise." (Luke 23:43)*

❧

While Jesus was hanging on the cross, he was not alone. A
crowd surrounded him, his killers insulted him, followers gathered alongside him, and there were two other executions
happening next to him. He was hung between two thieves. Jesus
addressed one of them while dying. He said, "Today you will be
with me in paradise" (Luke 23:43). Why? What was going on
when he said that? Of all the things Jesus could have said, and all
the people he could have spoken to, why expend precious energy
to say that to a thief? The man was not strung up for shoplifting,
but for robbery. He was most likely a repeat offender. The state
was making an example out of him. Why then did Jesus offer this
promise of paradise?

JERUSALEM

To answer the question why, let's go back to the setting and try to understand the mind of the common person in Jesus's day in Jerusalem. Jerusalem was bustling because it was Passover. Passover was a time of celebration and remembering, a week to reflect on how God freed his people from Egypt long ago. The first Passover was the tipping point where slavery, tyranny, and abuse came to its end. Times had changed. Centuries later, people longed for the good old days of independence, stability, and strength of God's kingdom. In Luke we read "they supposed that the kingdom of God was to appear immediately" (Luke 19:11), but Rome was presently the kingdom in control. Israel had not had political independence for centuries. Taxes were high. The mood was oppressive. One way to control people was through brutal public punishments like executions on crosses, the torturous instruments of death placed on hills for all to see.

The Passover celebration taking place in Jerusalem recounted events surrounding the tenth plague described in Exodus 12. At the time of the plague, every family was to take a lamb, kill it, and put the blood on the top and sides of their door frame. They were to eat all of the lamb that night. They would raise, feed, and protect each lamb until it was time to kill it. These were real bleating, bucking, hopping, and walking lambs. This meal took preparation and death.

What was the point of all this slaughter? It was an act of faith for people who had no hope except in their God. The lambs died so that people would live. The angel of death spared God's people because of the lambs that were slain on that first Passover. God substituted the animals for the people.

God did not tolerate sin. He'd had enough of Pharaoh's obstinacy at that original Passover. He warned Pharaoh of the impending judgment and death sentence for his disobedience.

Pharaoh's heart was hard. The angel of death passed over Israel, giving them reprieve in the land of Goshen. Israel was safe from the destroyer; Egypt was not.

But times change—or do they? Now Rome was in power instead of Egypt. Who could overthrow the tyranny of the elite? Who could break the bonds of the power brokers and right the wrongs of the evildoers? The protection Rome offered was only a guise for extortion. They were not fooling anyone. Rome did not care about people. Most everyone knew it. Life was not much better than it was back in Egypt. Times were tough, taxes were high, savings were meager, and health was fragile. Israel was hoping for relief again, remembering God's provision a millennium and a half before.

Do you long for relief? Do you feel oppressed? Work, school, or home can all put pressure on us so that we look for an out. You may seek a new employer or to be self-employed, a new school, or just an escape. Life is hard. The Jewish people had hard lives. They were hoping for freedom and help. Do you know that feeling? That was the feeling in the air during the Passover week in Jerusalem.

MESSIAH

Jerusalem gathered people from all over the known world. The market and temple were astir. A rumor buzzed in the air like flies on roadkill: the Messiah was in town—at least, some thought he was the Messiah. They wondered if the prophecies of the Old Testament were about this man. Moses had talked about a coming prophet who would speak God's words (Deuteronomy 18:15–19). God had promised David a descendant king who would have an everlasting throne and God as his father (2 Samuel 7:12–16). Isaiah had foretold a virgin birth and a child called "Wonderful Counselor, Everlasting Father, Mighty God, Prince of Peace"

(Isaiah 9:6–7). The people wondered if Jesus was the prophesied one entering Jerusalem.

The Messiah would bring justice to the nations, sight to the blind, freedom for the captives, and light to the world (Isaiah 42:1–7). Well, Jesus healed the blind. He said he was the light (John 8:12). The people shouted, "Hosanna! to the Son of David! Blessed is he who comes in the name of the Lord! Hosanna in the highest!" (Matthew 21:9). Palm branches and cloaks went to the ground in honor of him. His entrance echoed a prophetic prediction in Zechariah: "Rejoice greatly, O daughter of Zion! Shout aloud, O daughter of Jerusalem! Behold, your king is coming to you; righteous and having salvation is he, humble and mounted on a donkey, on a colt, the foal of a donkey" (Zechariah 9:9). The word spread. I can imagine people saying, "He is in town! The time has come! The time is now!" Maybe this would be the year of the turning of the tables, casting off the shackles of Roman rule, the coming of the Lord, and the hope of the ages.

I think we can relate to the yearning of the people. In our hearts, you and I want relief too. Think of your deepest desires. We want better days and better government. We see corruption and injustice and want change. Jesus's arrival was electrifying. It seems like everyone wanted him to be the answer. However, things didn't go as the people planned. All this excitement set the stage for a tragic disappointment. Jesus entered as a king and was killed as a criminal before the week was out. So much for hope. But in his last words to a thief next to him, we get a promise of the hope we really need and they didn't anticipate.

A THIEF'S MIND

The week passed quickly. Friday was a good day for death with the Sabbath coming. It would be unlawful to execute on the Sabbath. The thieves next to Jesus probably hoped something might change about their impending sentence. The government had a tradition that each year the public could choose one criminal could get pardoned. Perhaps they thought, "It could be me." I imagine hearts raced and hoped and anticipated this. But whom do the people choose? They chose Barabbas, a rabble-rouser, and rebel. He was no saint; he was a thug. Why release Barabbas? Why not release Christ or even a crook? It did not make sense.

We don't know all the thoughts of the thieves that day. Their minds probably bounced between hope and despair. Where do your thoughts go under pressure? Where is your hope when all seems lost? How do you deal with distress? In the midst of crisis, keeping thoughts clear can be impossible.

Probably the outlaws regretted their crimes or at least wished they hadn't been caught. Do you have regrets? I have heard some say, "I have no regrets. I would do it all over again." For those who think that way, what if you could change one small thing: silence a hurtful word, stop yourself from giving in, or take initiative where you neglected doing the right thing? Would you take another course of action? I imagine in those moments of execution, many *what-ifs* flew through those criminals' minds.

Sometimes, under trial we excuse ourselves and shift the blame. It was someone else's fault: our parents, our birth order, our personality, our lack of opportunity, our friends, or God. Perhaps the thieves were tempted to pin their actions on someone else. That is a common coping mechanism used to protect oneself.

Suffering has a way of focusing us on self-preservation. Suffering consumes us. Our problem-solving frequently moves us toward introspection. But in Jesus's time of trouble he did the opposite. He prayed that God would forgive his tormentors. Maybe Jesus's mercy moved the heart of the thief to make his appeal. Maybe it was Jesus's silence to his accusers that got the criminal's attention. Maybe this thief was aware of Jesus's ministry and teaching.

Visualize yourself as this thief, for a moment. Jesus turns his face in your direction and your eyes meet. While a placard above him mockingly says he is the King of the Jews, blood drips down his face from a crown of thorns. Pain, exhaustion, and sorrow lingers behind his gaze. Notice something else. He sees you and knows you as you hang there dying with him. He looks into you. He doesn't look through you. He sees your soul.

Continue to put yourself in those moments and hear this interruption of thought:

> The rulers scoffed at him, saying, "He saved others; let him save himself, if he is the Christ of God, his Chosen One!" The soldiers also mocked him, coming up and offering him sour wine and saying, "If you are the King of the Jews, save yourself!" (Luke 23:35–37)

An innocent man was dying next to criminals, yet the innocent one was being verbally attacked, not the criminals. As if the crucifixion were not enough of a cosmic tragedy, the leaders and executioners were ridiculing the God who made them and sustained their existence. They had no idea who they were talking to. The jeering continued. The other thief spoke, lashing out at Jesus, "Are you not the Christ? Save yourself and us!" (Luke 23:39). The criminal's derision was that of a bully. It was not a humble question or gentle request. His words were weaponized with a perverted pleasure to strike Jesus once more. This was a demonic taunt aimed to wound.

Hearing all this, how would you respond? Have you ever defended a person from verbal attack? Have you spoken up for the weak? What was that like for you?

The first thief responded to his comrade's hurtful words. He rebuked him, saying, "Do you not fear God, since you are under the same sentence of condemnation? And we indeed justly, for we are receiving the due reward of our deeds; but this man has done nothing wrong" (Luke 23:40–41). Nothing wrong! That is a statement of faith. The thief understood better than most that day. Jesus didn't deserve verbal abuse, let alone death.

We know Jesus came into this world as a baby and did nothing wrong his whole life. He left this world condemned and murdered for doing good. He never lied, never stole, and never took a life. Jesus never undressed a woman with his eyes. He never cut a person down to make himself feel better. He never stuffed himself with food to escape the bother or boredom of life, or drank to get drunk, or disobeyed his parents. He never stared at himself in the mirror to admire how great he looked. He never gossiped or slandered. He never cheated, took revenge, or sabotaged a project for promotion. He was perfect. He *is* perfect. He had done nothing wrong—nothing. The thief's defense was a strong statement of truth: in a sense, he confessed that he had done wrong and Jesus had not.

What wrong have you done? In chapter 1 we explored forgiveness and saw God's heart of mercy in light of our debt to God. The thief longed for that forgiveness Jesus prayed about. He was in the most hopeless situation imaginable, but longed for mercy in the life to come. He turned to Jesus and made a request: "Jesus, remember me when you come into your kingdom" (v. 42). That was an act of faith, like putting blood on the doorposts was so many centuries earlier. Do you hear the hope and yearning in his voice?

As you put yourself there, what would you seek? Do you see that Jesus has done nothing wrong? Do you believe he is who he said he is? Do you yearn for his help? What do you seek from God?

Jesus answered, "Truly, I say to you, today you will be with me in paradise" (v. 43). *Today you will be with me.* I can imagine the thief's eyes welling up with tears. What a gift! What a vision of a future that would be radically different than anything he had ever known. Paradise! Jesus's word was better than Israel's political revival. It was better than lower taxes or a lottery payout. It was a promise of hope for one whose situation was hopeless. Consider the juxtaposition of paradise and punishment on that hill. Only Jesus could make a statement like this and have it be real. He was the Messiah, the Christ. He was saving people from their sins, including this thief. Jesus was the lamb slain to take away the sin of the world—and the sin of this thief. He really said and meant *today you will be with me in paradise.* Yes, Jesus was the King of the Jews, the King of kings, and Lord of lords, and King of this man before him. Jesus had done nothing wrong; instead, he continued to do good to a dying thief at his side.

YOUR PARDON

In those moments, Jesus was speaking a promise that our hearts need. Looking at this second saying of Christ on the cross we find that Jesus's words offer hope. If at the last hour a guilty thief could find mercy, we can as well. The thief was never baptized or catechized. He would not memorize Scripture, walk an aisle, pray pious prayers, or win a service award. He did what needed to be done: he turned to Jesus in faith for help. He acknowledged who Jesus was and made a request concerning his greatest need. He expressed his trust, and Jesus promised him paradise.

What do you struggle with these days? What do you desire deep in your soul? What baggage do you carry? Look Jesus in the eye at the cross. Speak the thief's words aloud as your own: *Jesus, remember me when you come into your kingdom.* Hear Jesus's words back: *Today you will be with me.* Today most likely is not the day of your homecoming to paradise, but the Bible says we can be with him now through the Spirit. He gives the Holy Spirit to all who truly believe (Romans 8:9). The means of our future entrance into paradise is granted through faith in him, by grace (Ephesians 2:8–9).

Our sins are forgiven, like the thief's, when we offer such a confession. The Bible says, "If we confess our sins, he is faithful and just to forgive us our sins and to cleanse us from all unrighteousness" (1 John 1:9). *All* unrighteousness is forgiven, not just some. Paradise is in sight. Paul the apostle wrote, "For the wages of sin is death, but the free gift of God is eternal life in Christ Jesus our Lord" (Romans 6:23). Eternal life is free to you because Jesus paid the ultimate price at the cross. Do you long for eternal life and paradise? Then believe! Do you desire forgiveness, peace with God, and his presence? Then believe! However sinful and hopeless your situation may seem, confess and believe, and hear Jesus's word to the thief as words to you. *Today you will be with me in paradise.*

REFLECTION

Take some time to reflect now on the hope that is yours, today, in Jesus:

See Your Need. The thief was in a desperate situation. Consider a time you were hopeless. Why was that? In what ways can you relate to the thief today? What do you long for right now?

See Jesus. Jesus spoke directly to the thief's request, stating that he would be with him in paradise. What assurance does Jesus's word to the thief offer you? Picture Jesus responding to your desperate longings. What goes on in your heart and mind hearing Jesus's words to you?

Come Near to God. Jesus promised the thief relief and friendship in his approaching death. What other promises in Scripture do you recall that offer comfort (for example, in Hebrews 13:5 God says, "I will never leave you or forsake you")? God is trustworthy, and his promises are true. As you think of your longings, what helps you hold on to faith in God in trials? How might you cling to God's character and the truth of his Word during the day (for example, memorizing a verse, or singing a song)?

Go to Others. In what ways might having an eternal hope change how you interact with those who don't know this promise? Whom might you talk with about what God offers us? When and how might that happen in the coming weeks?

Pray.

> God, I fall short of my expectations, goals, dreams, desires, and hopes at times. Honestly, I fall short of what you desire. Perfection slips from my grasp like water through my hands. Sin is closer than my neighbor. Temptation is beside me. Forgive me for my sins, please. Thank you for the death of your Son. I hurl my prayer for mercy as the thief did to you. Remember me. I hope in you. Thank you for your faithfulness and promises. Help me to share who you are and what you have done with those around me. Thank you for Good Friday and your words of hope.

3

Behold

"Woman, behold, your son!" Then he said to the disciple,
"Behold, your mother!" (John 19:26–27)

❧

We have seen Jesus's heart of mercy and compassion for the masses and the individual. Jesus looked to his Father and sought forgiveness for those who did not know what they were doing, and offered hope to the penitent man next to him. He was not done ministering even as he was dying. He was not done thinking of others even as he suffered.

His mother was there, weeping and watching. His beloved disciple John was there as well. Jesus said to them, "'Woman, behold, your son!' Then he said to the disciple, 'Behold, your mother!'" (John 19:26–27). I think we understand care for one's mother and we understand friendship, but John was not Mary's son, and Mary was not John's mother. What was Jesus doing? Why did he say that? Does it matter? I argue it does.

MOTHERS AND COMPASSION

Kids should not die in front of their parents. Yet on that Good Friday, Mary's son's life was ebbing away. As a child, she had held him. Her hugs and love would be instinctual to a mom. Her baby must have laughed, cried, and chattered. He would learn to crawl, walk, speak, grow, and develop as children do. She witnessed it all. Mary would have cared for him and nurtured him until he became a man. On his first visit to Jerusalem with his mother, a stranger approached, an old man known for being righteous and devout. This man had prayed for this moment to come. He dreamed to see the Messiah, the Promised One, the Son of God, the Lord's Christ. He spotted Mary. They met. He spoke a prophetic word: "Behold, this child is appointed for the fall and rising of many in Israel, and for a sign that is opposed (and a sword will pierce through your own soul also)" (Luke 2:34–35). The rising and falling and piercing. Mary was used to pronouncements. Angelic encounters, a virgin birth, expensive gifts from wise men—she knew Jesus was no ordinary child. But what did Simeon mean? Sword?

I am sure she remembered and felt that blade as Jesus died. The sharp edge of reality ripped through her soul as the Pharisees and Romans murdered her son when he had done nothing wrong. The weeping and tears must have blinded her and run dry in her heartache. Her son did not deserve this. She could only watch and weep and pray. He suffered among criminals. This was not a "Good Friday" for Mary.

As time passed, he moved closer and closer and closer to death. His life drained before her eyes. Unbelievably, he prayed for God to forgive his tormentors. Then he promised paradise to a criminal. Now he turned to her and his disciple, John. What did he say? "Woman, behold, your son!" (John 19:26). He acknowledged her and gave her a gift. He consoled her with words that meant something in a male-dominated society. He knew what she needed and offered some comfort. John could provide financially and emotionally the support of a son to an aging widow. Jesus couldn't take away the searing pain of having to watch him die, but he could help as her firstborn son. Consolation.

What consolation do you need? What pain do you carry? You and I suffer. Life and trials go hand in hand. Jesus saw it and experienced it. He knew tribulation. He saw his own difficulty and yours. He knew his mother's weakness. He was not consumed with himself when we could be, but looked out and offered comfort to others, to those distant and close. That is what his first few words communicate to us. They portray Jesus's heart of compassion.

JOHN

Jesus turned to John and offered a similar gift: "Behold, your mother" (John 19:27).

Why? Remember the context. John was part of Jesus's inner circle. He was one of Jesus's closest friends. However, Jesus's words may have come as a surprise. John was not a son of Mary, and Mary had other children. After Jesus, there were four more sons, to be exact (Matthew 13:55 lists them). However, none of them were followers yet and were likely not present.

In ancient times family ties were thick. Responsibility fell on the sons to take on the family business and care for their aging parents. That is what the apostle Paul taught in 1 Timothy 5:3–8. Sons were the ones inheriting, perpetuating, and supporting the family. Mary's sons could have taken care of her. So, why does Jesus make this comment to his mother and John?

Jesus had an even bigger view of family than the prevailing culture. In Matthew 12:46–50, Jesus flipped the understanding of family on its head. Jesus's mother and brothers came to visit.

Those around him thought he would want to see them right away. He used their interruption as a teaching point that those who do his will are his mother and brothers. He was teaching that the spiritual family is more important. John was part of that spiritual family and so was Mary. They were followers of Jesus. Jesus seemed to be saying that belonging to the family of God is more precious and important than even our ties to our earthly families.

At the cross, Jesus first spoke of forgiveness, pointing us to our forgiveness found in his death. Then he spoke salvation to a thief, reminding us, he died to save. Here he speaks to his mother and friend, communicating they are family. They are part of a larger spiritual family, the family of faith, reminding us of the fact that Jesus died to bring us into the family of God. This is the perfect and better family we each long for.

The surprise that Jesus spoke to John is even bigger than biology and this spiritual reality of the brotherhood and sisterhood of believers. Remember the context. John was a coward. He had abandoned Jesus hours before at his greatest point of need (Mark 14:50). Yet, Jesus assigns him one of the most honored tasks, taking care of his mother. The sweet comfort and honor of having Jesus's mother as your own at such a time of sorrow was tremendous. This was a marvelous gift.

Jesus's words offered peace and kindness to a friend who probably felt the weight of guilt over his betrayal. I imagine his burden of shame felt like drowning or being run over slowly by a half-ton truck. All of the sudden, Jesus's adoption notice offered relief and comfort. I think it was much like the promise of paradise to the thief. It was a word of grace.

What word of grace do you need? Where do you seek comfort? Who can you talk to or process with? Who helps you through difficulties? Maybe you are tough and try to go it alone.

Maybe you are an island, tower, or fighter. You don't want to get close to anyone—you have been burned too many times. Maybe you don't feel weak. John's world was imploding before him, yet Jesus's word extends comfort. His Savior, Teacher, Master, and Lord was ministering to him in a deep and personal way with a few words amid his own suffering.

WHAT WE LEARN

What do you hear in Jesus's words? He died to forgive and express his extravagant affection and mercy. He gives us a window into his heart. Jesus was a comforter to the end. His heart was one of grace and love.

Was this only a private conversation between three people? No. Jesus offers us love and comfort too. All who truly believe are united by faith to one another through the extravagant love of our Lord. We are part of God's family, "fellow citizens with the saints and members of the household of God" (Ephesians 2:19). We are the body of Christ on earth (Romans 12:5). We are brothers and sisters to each other spiritually. We are made for community. We may not all be extroverts, but we need each other. We need the comfort found in a spiritual community made possible through Christ's death and echoed in Jesus's gift to Mary and John.

Jesus comforts. He offered this to his followers, and to us as well:

> "Come to me, all who labor and are heavy laden, and I will give you rest. Take my yoke upon you, and learn from me, for I am gentle and lowly in heart, and you will find rest for your souls. For my yoke is easy, and my burden is light." (Matthew 11:28–30)

REFLECTION

Are you heavy laden? Do you have a weight around your neck and feel like you are drowning? Jesus cares. He loves you literally to death. He turned his thoughts from himself and his problems to his frail mother and fickle friend. See how his comfort to them is a comfort to you. Before we move on, reflect on this:

See Your Need. Are you suffering like a sword has pierced your soul? How can you relate to Mary's grief? Where have you been cowardly like John in your faith? Where are you weak? How have you distanced yourself from Jesus's comfort or sought consolation outside of God?

See Jesus. Picture the heart behind Jesus's word to his mother and John. What is most shocking and uplifting about his compassion and consolation to you?

Come Near to God. Our Lord sees your deepest need. Where could you use Jesus's comfort in your life? What does it mean for you to be adopted into God's family? How might you press in toward his comfort in practical ways this week (for example, prayer, Bible reading, or specific spiritual disciplines)?

Go to Others. Second Corinthians 1:3–4 teaches that God comforts us so that we may comfort others. Who are the people in your life who are hurting? Write those names down on paper. How can you follow Jesus's example and show compassion to them in their pain and sorrow amidst your own pain and sorrow? List some ways you can minister to them during the next few weeks.

Pray.

God, thank you for all you have done in my life and history. I am a needy person. My heart aches for relief. I struggle, hunger, long, yearn, and want so much. I confess that my desires focus on me. Thank you for loving me while I was still a sinner. Thank you for expressing your love to your mother in the middle of your pain. Thank you for your love for your friend, John. I am amazed at your compassion during personal crises. Open my eyes to your compassion and love for me. Help me to extend that love to others. Help me to know your compassion and have your compassion. Thank you for Good Friday.

4

Why

"My God, my God, why have you forsaken me?"
(Matthew 27:46)

❧

Jesus's previous words demonstrated his caring heart. He was merciful, forgiving, and compassionate at a point where we would be screaming for it all to stop. The next word he spoke on the cross was different: it was a word vocalizing the torment he endured. Like the first word, he spoke again to God. However, he lost the intimacy of calling him Father and only calls him God. He cried out, "My God, my God, why have you forsaken me?" (Matthew 27:46). The wisest person ever to have lived, Jesus, died asking God a question. The Son of God asked God the Father a question.

Prophesies, like Isaiah 53, had predicted the Servant of God would suffer. Jesus himself had predicted it too again and again. He had prayed the night before, asking the Father to remove the cup of wrath he was going to drink. Jesus knew what was happening. He didn't have to ask. So why the question?

THE MOUTH OF THE LION

The key to understanding Jesus's question is to understand a Hebrew poem from a thousand years before he spoke. This poem was penned in that same arid land. It was a riddle locked in papyrus until the day Jesus died. The author of that poem was the shepherd boy David. He not only played and composed music, he slew the giant Goliath. Overnight, he became a national superstar. Israel's King Saul eventually elevated him from musician to control some of Israel's army.

Given to depression, impulsivity, and self-centered tendencies, Saul turned on David. When a scheme to get David killed in battle failed, Saul took a direct approach. He randomly threw spears at David to kill him. In angry fits, possibly drunk with wine, but surely drunk with rage, he attempted murder again and again.

David went on the run. He hid. He pretended to be crazy in front of enemies. He found comfort in the company of scoundrels. He lived in the wilderness. Where was God in all of that? Why did David have to suffer? We don't know if he ever got a direct answer from God about such questions, but we do know that he wondered as much. Psalm 22 is one of David's poems probably written during this struggle with Saul. It begins,

> My God, my God, why have you forsaken me?
>> Why are you so far from saving me, from the words of
>> my groaning?
> O my God, I cry by day, but you do not answer,
>> and by night, but I find no rest. (Psalm 22:1–2)

Does that sound familiar? This passage articulates a troubled heart and a desire for answers. It is exactly what Jesus quoted on the cross. Yes, Jesus was quoting the psalms of David as he died. Verses 19 through 21 state something along those same lines:

> But you, O LORD, do not be far off!
>> O you my help, come quickly to my aid!
> Deliver my soul from the sword,
>> my precious life from the power of the dog!
> Save me from the mouth of the lion!

On the cross, Jesus was praying Psalm 22. God seemed distant. God the Father abandoned Jesus to suffer alone. How could that be if Jesus is God the Son and his Father is God? I think this mystery of the Trinity is understood in the word *forsaking*. This forsaking was an experience of God the Father's wrath for the sin of the world from the beginning to end—fully vented on Jesus, God's Son, all at once. This does not mean divinity was divided or Jesus ceased to be God, so there is some mystery in how this happened. Yet it was a clear punishment, suffered by the person Jesus in his human nature, intended for the sin of the world. This was the worst pain ever. Ever.

Jesus had not slept the night before. He had not eaten. He was made fun of, beaten, tried, sentenced to death, betrayed by friends, and now punished by the Father. Psalm 22 expresses his torment prophetically: "I cry by day, but you do not answer, and by night, but I find no rest." Reading further, the psalm details more than coincidental connections to Jesus's experience. It was a prediction being fulfilled for the world to see.

> Yet you are holy,
>> enthroned on the praises of Israel.
> In you our fathers trusted;
>> they trusted, and you delivered them.

To you they cried and were rescued;
>in you they trusted and were not put to shame.
But I am a worm and not a man,
>scorned by mankind and despised by the people.
All who see me mock me;
>they make mouths at me; they wag their heads;
"He trusts in the LORD; let him deliver him;
>let him rescue him, for he delights in him!" (vv. 3–8)

This passage predicted Jesus's persecution, his being treated like a worm and not a man. It predicted the scorning, despising, and rejecting. The psalm continues to parallel Christ's death in striking ways. It refers to Jesus's mother, and his subsequent word of thirst, and poetically expresses the tribulations he endured.

Yet you are he who took me from the womb;
>you made me trust you at my mother's breasts.
On you was I cast from my birth,
>and from my mother's womb you have been my God.
Be not far from me,
>for trouble is near,
>and there is none to help.
Many bulls encompass me;
>strong bulls of Bashan surround me;
they open wide their mouths at me,
>like a ravening and roaring lion.
I am poured out like water,
>and all my bones are out of joint;
my heart is like wax;
>it is melted within my breast;
my strength is dried up like a potsherd,
>and my tongue sticks to my jaws.
>you lay me in the dust of death. (vv. 9–15)

Jesus's tongue must have stuck to his mouth. He thirsted as he hung there. He told us so, minutes after he made this comment. Remember Jesus's location. He was in the Middle East, at the height of the day, impaled on a tree. He was sweating and bleeding. He had no water. He thirsted.

> For dogs encompass me;
>> a company of evildoers encircles me;
> they have pierced my hands and feet—
> I can count all my bones—
> they stare and gloat over me;
> they divide my garments among them,
>> and for my clothing they cast lots. (vv. 16–18)

Evildoers encircled Jesus. They pierced his hands and feet. They gloated over him. They cast lots for his clothes. This was not a gloss to make it look like Psalm 22 predicted what would happen after the fact. Psalm 22 was written a thousand years before. The apostles didn't make this up after the fact either. No credible counter-argument survives about Jesus's death. The ancient secular historian Josephus even acknowledged Jesus died by crucifixion. The disciples gave their lives for this truth. Jesus was fulfilling Psalm 22, and that is a fact.

Understanding this prophetic reality Jesus was fulfilling doesn't answer his own question. Why? Why did he suffer? Why was he forsaken?

RECEIVING WRATH FOR THE SAKE OF JOY

God's answer circles back to how, even in this horrible event, he was in control. The cross was not "plan B." The cross was God's plan before all time. In Genesis 3:15, God promised to crush a serpent, the devil, with a descendant from Eve. Jesus was that descendant.

How did Jesus fulfill this prophecy? He experienced the hell we deserve when he was forsaken. This was not like any other death before or since. The betrayal of friends, the mocking of the Son of God, the trumped-up charges, the slaps in the face while blindfolded, the scourging, and the anguish of being nailed naked on a beam to suffocate were not the worst part of Good Friday. The most horrible experience Jesus suffered was God's wrath on him for our rebellion. The penalty for every evil deed, each wicked thought, and all sinful words of those who were children of God and would become children of God by faith in Jesus was experienced in those dying breaths.

Jesus knew that. He chose to endure God's wrath. The Bible tells us Jesus embraced his death with a long perspective of joy: "For the joy that was set before him [he] endured the cross, despising the shame" (Hebrews 12:2). Jesus looked past the monstrosity of being forsaken to see the results of his sacrifice, the righting of wrongs, the straightening of the crooked, the hope for the sinner, and the glory of God's radical love on display for all to see. At the cross, we hear Psalm 22 echoed and see the Son forsaken—so we would never be. God will never forsake you and me.

Jesus was well aware of Psalm 22. It doesn't end in darkness. It continues. Interestingly, Psalm 22 promises triumph through tragedy:

> You have rescued me from the horns of the wild oxen!
> I will tell of your name to my brothers;
>> in the midst of the congregation I will praise you:
> You who fear the LORD, praise him!
>> All you offspring of Jacob, glorify him,
>> and stand in awe of him, all you offspring of Israel!

For he has not despised or abhorred
> the affliction of the afflicted,
and he has not hidden his face from him,
> but has heard, when he cried to him.
From you comes my praise in the great congregation;
> my vows I will perform before those who fear him.
The afflicted shall eat and be satisfied;
> those who seek him shall praise the LORD!
> May your hearts live forever! (vv. 21–26)

As these phrases likely zipped through Jesus's mind, he knew the outcome of his offering. Reading the closing verses of Psalm 22 now, make sure you don't just skim past them. Read them carefully. Perhaps even read them aloud. Trust me on this one. It will help the words sink in and answer Jesus's question.

All the ends of the earth shall remember
> and turn to the LORD,
and all the families of the nations
> shall worship before you.
For kingship belongs to the LORD,
> and he rules over the nations.
All the prosperous of the earth eat and worship;
> before him shall bow all who go down to the dust,
> even the one who could not keep himself alive.
Posterity shall serve him;
> it shall be told of the Lord to the coming generation;
they shall come and proclaim his righteousness to a people
> yet unborn,
> that he has done it. (Psalm 22:27–31)

This poem ends with promises made real by Jesus's death and resurrection. By faith in Jesus you have been, or can be, part of "the families of the nations" who worship him. You are his posterity. You are one of those who bow down. You are the coming generation predicted three thousand years ago. You are the proclaimers. You are the ones yet unborn. Jesus thought of you. He knew you before you were born. He cares about you. He died for you. He experienced a punishment and alienation so you would never have to.

As we recall the darkness of the day, reflect on Jesus's question and remember that he experienced what we never have to. The creation tried to kill the Creator on that Good Friday. It was a plan made before all time. God knew what he was doing and what would happen. The true King and true Lord suffered and bled for the expansion of worship to every tribe, tongue, and nation throughout history—including yours. God was making worship happen across the world and time, enduring the pain of the cross.

REFLECTION

This worship, forgiveness, and peace with God began with a forsaking. Weep and mourn with those early followers over your sin. Feel the desolation and depression of Christ's punishment on your behalf. Reflect on the atrocity he endured. He embraced the Father's wrath so you would never have to. You are loved that much! He experienced that for you!

See Your Need. In what ways does Psalm 22 resonate with your life? Have you ever felt like God abandoned you? Jesus felt forsaken; when have you felt forsaken by God? What was that experience like for you?

See Jesus. What parts about Jesus's suffering on the cross and his living out Psalm 22 strike you as meaningful? How would you explain to someone not familiar with the cross what Jesus endured and why he endured it? Spend some time reflecting on the glorious truth that because Jesus was forsaken in your place, you never will be.

Come Near to God. How might you express your gratitude and praise to God for embracing judgment, punishment, and wrath on your behalf (you could make a list, tell someone, journal)? Take a moment to express thanks to God for Christ's suffering in your place.

Go to Others. When God seems distant, how aware are you of others' suffering and needs? Pain can eclipse our ability to see our neighbor and offer ministry. As you consider the extent of Christ's love for you, are there those in your life who need care but you have been neglecting? What could you do to reach out to them this week? What might it look like to go to a great length to extend God's love them this month? How can you help carry their burden?

Pray.

God, I have known abandonment, loneliness, and confusion, but I don't know nor will I ever know exactly what Jesus experienced on that day. Thank you for sending your Son to a place I never have to go. Thank you that he was forsaken so I won't be. Thank you for the cross. Thank you for hope. Thank you for your sovereign reign and rule that has a plan and a love for me. Thank you for hope amid suffering. Help me in my trials, and turn my gaze to you. Help me hang on to you, knowing you took the penalty for my sin. Give me the insight and ability to love my neighbor as you loved me. Thank you for Good Friday.

5

Thirst

"I thirst." (John 19:28)

❧

We have seen how Jesus was thinking of others as he died, yet he suffered greatly. Innocently, he bore the weight of the world's sin, dying the death of a criminal. In his fifth saying on the cross, he said, "I thirst" (John 19:28). What significance can we unearth from a simple, two-word statement?

We all need water. It makes up about sixty percent of our bodies.* We can only live so long without it. It is a building block of life, including Jesus's life here on earth. We are thirsty people. In his two words, "I thirst," he expressed his humanity. He was fully one of us. Those two words connect us to him.

The perfect God became completely, simultaneously, and incomprehensibly God and man in one person. Born of Mary, he nursed in infancy. Weaned, he quenched his thirst with water from the promised land. The land flowing with milk and honey sustained him. Luke 2:40 says, he "grew and became strong,

---

* "The Water in You: Water and the Human Body," website of the U.S. Geological Survey; Water Science School, updated May 22, 2019, https://water.usgs.gov/edu/propertyyou.html.

filled with wisdom." We don't know much about the details of his childhood or young adulthood, but we see his life began like it ended, with thirst. He was fully one of us. His humanity was essential. Why? The answer is connected to his purpose, seen in his ministry.

SATISFYING THE SOUL'S THIRST

Let me ask you this: "What do you thirst after?" You and I hunger and thirst for food and drink, sure. But what else do you thirst after? Do you long for someone to understand you? Do you seek meaning and purpose? Do you desire friendship and companionship? Do you want answers, help, comfort, security, safety, control, happiness, pleasure, or ease? You and I seek so many things, don't we? Sometimes we find satisfaction, but any satisfaction we experience is fleeting. The friend moves away. Our healthy family is disrupted by a sudden diagnosis. The children who are doing so well socially start straying and making decisions we know are going to result in heartache. We see sin's effects all around, from droughts to floods, from pollution to contamination, from hurt to rebellion resident in our souls, so that all of creation "waits with eager longing for the revealing of the sons of God" (Romans 8:19). Meanwhile, we all thirst.

Jesus began his ministry quenching thirst. His first miracle was at a party foreshadowing the result of the cross by literally satisfying thirsts. He transformed one hundred and fifty gallons of wash water into fine wine after a host's embarrassment of running out at the wedding at Cana. That miracle made a statement. It was celebratory. It was an announcement of another wedding approaching: God and man were united in one person, Jesus, and through his life, death, and resurrection he would purchase another union—the union of God and his church. This drink symbolized the overflow of grace Jesus would extend to the world, you, and me. The party guests at Cana were thirsty and Jesus satisfied them. He cared about thirst.

He cared about satisfying the thirst of the poor. He taught that whoever gives a cup of cold water to the least significant person, in his name, was giving it to him (Matthew 25:40). He cared about the marginalized and those on the fringe. He knew people's physical needs and met them time and time again. He shared, listened, encouraged, defended, and loved the outcast. He gave the disciples a mission to emulate: Jesus cared for the physical thirsts.

He cared about the spiritual as well as the physical. In arguably the greatest message ever given, the Sermon on the Mount, Jesus taught that whoever hungers and thirsts after righteousness will be satisfied (Matthew 5:6). How? On our own, we don't have rightness and purity before God. So how can we quench the thirst of our souls?

Jesus cried out the answer to that question at the Feast of Tabernacles: "If anyone thirsts, let him come to me and drink. Whoever believes in me, as the Scripture has said, 'Out of his heart will flow rivers of living water'" (John 7:37–38). Jesus satisfies the soul's thirst. We need only to believe in him, to come to him, to quench our thirst.

WATER THAT LASTS

Another time Jesus spoke of satisfying thirst was as he passed a well in Samaria, north of Jerusalem. He was thirsty. A Samaritan woman was gathering water. She was thirsty too. In those days, men often did not talk to women, and Jewish men certainly didn't talk to Samaritans. However, Jesus looked past cultural taboos, sordid skeletons, and theological errors. He saw *her*. He saw her soul's thirst. He approached and made a simple request for a drink of water.

The Samaritan woman said to him, "How is it that you, a Jew, ask for a drink from me, a woman of Samaria?" (For Jews have no dealings with Samaritans.) Jesus answered her, "If you knew the gift of God, and who it is that is saying to you, 'Give me a drink,' you would have asked him, and he would have given you living water." The woman said to him, "Sir, you have nothing to draw water with, and the well is deep. Where do you get that living water? Are you greater than our father Jacob? He gave us the well and drank from it himself, as did his sons and his livestock."

Jesus said to her, "Everyone who drinks of this water will be thirsty again, but whoever drinks of the water that I will give him will never be thirsty again. The water that I will give him will become in him a spring of water welling up to eternal life." (John 4:9–14)

Jesus was offering this woman what he offered the crowd at the feast. He was offering to satisfy the soul's thirst forever. This is so satisfying that it will result in eternal life. Water sustains an earthly life; Jesus offers life forever. He is better than the fountain of youth; he is the fountain of eternal life.

How could he offer water that quenches thirst eternally? He answered that speaking to his disciples at the Last Supper. Jesus connected the Passover wine to his blood that he would shed hours later for the forgiveness of sin. His blood accomplished what he promised the crowd, the Samaritan woman, and the disciples. No other blood could do what Jesus's blood could.

He embraced his death as well as thirst. He was making a great exchange: one human for other humans, perfect for imperfect. Hebrews gives us an answer to why he thirsted: "Therefore he had to be made like his brothers in every respect, so that he might become a merciful and faithful high priest in the service of God, to make propitiation for the sins of the people" (Hebrews 2:17). Jesus was made like us in every respect. He thirsted as we thirst. He was human, yet perfect. He was merciful and faithful when we have not been. He was the great High Priest and at the same time the perfect sacrifice. He made propitiation: he took God's wrath on our behalf. Jesus's thirst flows from his humanity, and his humanity was essential for this exchange. He took our place. He was our substitute.

Jesus's thirst shows who he is, what we need, and how he met that need two thousand years ago. The dry cotton mouth sensation of dehydration was real. God truly became man with all his hunger and thirst that we might truly be united with him. He embraced humanity that we might enjoy the divinity eternally.

Isaiah the prophet predicted this. He gave an invitation from God that you and I can enjoy today, right now. We can come to Jesus and find a satisfaction for our thirst just like Jesus's disciples, the Samaritan woman, and the crowd at the feast. Isaiah says to you,

"Come, everyone who thirsts,
    come to the waters;
and he who has no money,
    come, buy and eat!
Come, buy wine and milk
    without money and without price.
Why do you spend your money for that which is not bread,
    and your labor for that which does not satisfy?
Listen diligently to me, and eat what is good,
    and delight yourselves in rich food.
Incline your ear, and come to me;
    hear, that your soul may live." (Isaiah 55:1–3)

REFLECTION

Do you thirst? Do you thirst *for God*? Do you long for forgiveness? Do you hunger for love and acceptance, peace and provision? Find your soul's satisfaction in God. Come to him and buy his wine and milk without price—at least without price to you. Good Friday was excruciating because we see a thirsty man die a horrendous death. However, Good Friday is good because you and I see our substitute. His tacky mouth is just one expression of his care for you. He understands you because he was like you in every respect. Take his offer, and satisfy your thirst in him today. Begin with some reflections on thirst:

See Your Need. Are you thirsty, spiritually, for God? Do you long for a better relationship with him? Do you feel alienated or estranged from him because of a secret sin? Have you been running to another source to satisfy thirsts that only God can satisfy? In what ways do you long for more of God in your life?

See Jesus. Jesus embraced his humanity to the point of death on the cross. He understands hunger, thirst, and temptation. He sympathizes with you. "For we do not have a high priest who is unable to sympathize with our weaknesses, but one who in every respect has been tempted as we are, yet without sin" (Hebrews 4:15). What physical or spiritual thirst do you have right now that Jesus had? How might his experience of that longing be a comfort to you?

Come Near to God. How can you draw near to God and his Word and find satisfaction for your soul's thirst this week? Is there a sin you need to give up? Is there a step of obedience you have been neglecting? Is God calling you to embrace a spiritual discipline to satisfy your thirst in him (like solitude, silence, or fasting)? Take a step toward quenching your spiritual thirst with God. Write that step down and commit to making it happen.

Go to Others. When Jesus satisfies our thirst, those around us will be impacted. He said, "Whoever believes in me, as the Scripture has said, 'Out of his heart will flow rivers of living water'" (John 7:38). How do you think God's fulfilling your spiritual thirsts could affect those around you? Who would it impact? How might God use your growth in godliness and holiness to bless others in the weeks ahead? Take a moment, and pray to God asking for insight into your answers to these questions.

Pray.

God, thank you for sending your Son as a man.
Thank you that he took my place. His thirst echoes
mine. I long for so much. My desires overwhelm me
from time to time. My expectations, dreams, and
goals are often unmet. I know disappointment. I
know you understand. I know you care. Your dry
mouth alone points to your affection for me. Thank
you. In my day-to-day thirsts, please satisfy me. In
my wanting, fill me. Make my heart at rest in you
and your ways, all my days. Help me to trust you,
enjoy you, and know you more. Show me how I
can find more of you. Use me to help other thirsty
sojourners find their thirsts satisfied in you. Thank
you for Good Friday.

6

Finished

"It is finished." (John 19:30)

◦❧◦

We are near the end of our journey through the last words of Christ. We have seen his mercy, compassion, selflessness, love, and humanity. He utters two more sentences. The one we look at now is profound: "When Jesus had received the sour wine, he said, 'It is finished,' and he bowed his head and gave up his spirit" (John 19:30). What was finished? Was it merely his life, or something more?

Scripture points to Jesus's death as the central event of all of history, defining the relationship between God and his people forever. The sacrifice of Jesus accomplished something extraordinary that has never happened before or since. Legends and myths echo what was realized on that day. History pivoted. A veil dividing the sacred and ordinary was torn and the earth shook. The universe will never be the same.

What do you want to be finished at the cross? Jesus's death has massive implications that extend beyond our wildest dreams. We find peace with God, forgiveness, affection, freedom, hope, and so much more. If we fully comprehend what Jesus meant by the words *It is finished,* our hearts naturally overflow with gratitude, worship, and obedience. Contemplate with me the meaning of the finished work of Christ.

THROUGH THE CROSS, JESUS TOOK OUR SIN

At the beginning of Jesus's ministry, John the Baptist told what the end of his ministry would mean. John announced, "Behold, the Lamb of God, who takes away the sin of the world!" (John 1:29; see also Isaiah 53:6, 11–12; Romans 6:23; 1 Corinthians 15:3; Hebrews 9:26, 28). When did Jesus take away the sin of the world? It was on the cross. He was the sacrificial lamb that God sent to take away our sins. John the Baptist foresaw that reality. That is what was finished on the cross. No other sacrifice is necessary. *"It is finished."*

Thousands of years before Jesus's death, God spared Abraham's one and only son with a sacrificial lamb. Passover, similarly, began when God passed over his people (held off his judgment) as they offered a sacrifice of spotless lambs (Exodus 12). That event was memorialized in a yearly sacrifice. All of them point to Christ's death. Jesus is the once-for-all sacrifice. He is the Lamb of God who takes away the sin of the world.

What sin do you need taken away? Through your faith in Christ, what he did took away your sin. When Jesus said, "It is finished," he took your jealousy, envy, greed, dissatisfaction, impatience, grumbling, lying, and deceiving. He took your lust of the eyes and the pride of life. He took your idolatrous exchanges where you worship God's gifts instead of him. He took your every faithless act, every wayward thought, and every careless word. He took your cheating, adultery, and perversity. He took your violence, rudeness, and unkindness. He took your selfishness, self-centeredness, and self-absorption. He took your gluttony, foolishness, and wickedness. He took not only your sins of doing the wrong things but the sins of not doing the right things. Every time you did not love, did not encourage, and did not speak up, he took those sins. He knows all your shortcomings because he took them. It was finished for you, believer, at the cross.

What does it mean that he took them? When he took your sins, he experienced your punishment on your behalf. He doesn't merely remove sins (theologians call that *expiation*); he experienced the penalty for them and experienced God's wrath (that is called *propitiation*) for them. You and I will never ever know that punishment because of what Jesus finished on the cross. Isaiah 53 predicted this long before Jesus's death:

> But he was pierced for our transgressions;
>   he was crushed for our iniquities;
> upon him was the chastisement that brought us peace,
>   and with his wounds we are healed. . . .
> Yet it was the will of the Lord to crush him;
>   he has put him to grief;
> when his soul makes an offering for guilt,
>   he shall see his offspring; he shall prolong his days;
> the will of the Lord shall prosper in his hand.
>   (Isaiah 53:5, 10)

All your guilt and shame are taken care of at the cross. All the fury connected to justice and your wrongdoing was spent on Jesus in those moments. If you confess your sins, repent, and trust in his finished work, then your guilt is gone.

Because of the finished work of Jesus, your past doesn't have to define you. Too often, people hang onto their past failures as their present identification. I frequently hear people are afraid to go to church because of their past. Their sin may have been decades old, and yet they feel it permanently marks them. They bear some type of scarlet letter. They think everyone is going to judge them. Paul writes, "If anyone is in Christ, he is a new creation" (2 Corinthians 5:17). Jesus took your sin at the cross. Walk in the light of what Jesus has done. He took your sin, all of it. Let Jesus's exchange put a spring in your step and smile on your face. You have a fresh start today because of the finished work of Christ through faith. Rejoice!

That is part of what Jesus meant when he said, "It is finished."

THROUGH THE CROSS, WE ARE FORGIVEN

The moment you are born is a moment closer to death. We are born with a terminal prognosis. We also inherit a spiritual ailment that destroys our relationships and jeopardizes the life beyond this one. Each day brings us nearer to the meeting of our maker and judgment.

Our malady is sin. It flows through our veins and is married to our humanity. Sin is a genetic flaw or ticking time bomb tethered to our body. However, we are not doomed to destruction. At the cross, God heals our spiritual infection and forgives us. Ephesians 1:7 says, "In him we have redemption through his blood, the forgiveness of our trespasses, according to the riches of his grace." As far as the east is from the west, God removes our sin from us and remembers it against us no more (Psalm 103:12).

What does that forgiveness look like? Imagine opening your mail today and finding a bill you had not anticipated. It is massive. The expense is beyond what you could ever hope to cover. You wish it was just a nightmare, but it is not. On top of that, there is no bailout or insurance to help you pay. Creditors won't let up or let it go. You are going to have to deal with collections. They will come after you and knock at your door and exact payment. You have no hope. What would go through your heart and mind if that was your reality? Maybe it is your reality.

Debt like that can be scary and depressing, but God talks about a spiritual debt that is even more disturbing. The debt owed to God for your rebellion is greater than any financial obligation you could incur. Jesus had to give his life for you to pay that debt off. How much is a life worth? As a parent, I would easily give up my life for my kids or wife. I would embrace death to save them. Their lives are priceless to me. How much more is the Son of God's life worth?

Colossians 2:13–14 says,

> And you, who were dead in your trespasses and the uncircumcision of your flesh, God made alive together with him, having forgiven us all our trespasses, by canceling the record of debt that stood against us with its legal demands. This he set aside, nailing it to the cross.

God canceled your spiritual debt with Jesus's life. Your ledger was wiped clean.

Jesus's finished work changes the way we view not only ourselves but others as well. Since Paul was able to say that he was the chief of sinners (1 Timothy 1:15), he had compassion on others who sinned. Being forgiven allows us to be forgiving and compassionate. This means that when our loved ones are trapped in sin, we can understand. When our bosses mistreat us, we can understand their broken-down logic. We understand how it is that a customer explodes on us or a classmate slanders us. They are stuck. We have been there. We too have been caught up in our sin. Grasping our spiritual debt and God's forgiveness empowers our ability to forgive others.

"It is finished." God has forgiven you who believe.

THROUGH THE CROSS, WE ARE REDEEMED

At the cross, Jesus paid the price necessary to get you back from a death row sentence. He bought you and owns you (see Galatians 3:13; Titus 2:14; Ephesians 1:7). Jesus redeemed you from that curse of the cross and your path of destruction. "You were ransomed from the futile ways inherited from your forefathers, not with perishable things such as silver or gold, but with the precious blood of Christ, like that of a lamb without blemish or spot" (1 Peter 1:18–19; see also 1 Timothy 2:5–6; Revelation 5:9; Psalm 49:7–9, 15; Hosea 13:14).

Speaking of his own purpose, Jesus said, "The Son of Man came not to be served but to serve, and to give his life as a ransom for many" (Matthew 20:28). We were all held hostage by the consequences of sin. We were slaves to our nature, the world, and darkness. Through Jesus's finished work, he paid the price for you to God.* He is your ransom, "obtained with his own blood" (Acts 20:28). You belong to God.

Do you hunger for belonging? Do you want to be known? Do you want to be part of something bigger? By grace through faith you are united to God through his Son's finished work on the cross. You do belong.

How? Your redemption is costly. Jesus gave up his body for you. He paid the price for your soul with his life, in a way no one else could. That blood price fuels devotion. A biblical response to his act of redemption is to turn around in joy and gratitude and to honor God in all you think, say, and do. We can glorify God with the big decisions in life and the little ones.

---

* For a discussion about to whom the ransom is paid, see Trevin Wax, "Christ Pays the Ransom, But to Whom?" website of The Gospel Coalition, January 30, 2014, blogs.thegospelcoalition.org/trevinwax/2014/01/30/christ-pays-the-ransom-but-to-whom/. The conclusion is that the ransom is paid to God.

When Jesus said, "It is finished," one more implication is redemption. He exchanged his life for yours.

THROUGH THE CROSS, WE ARE CLEANSED

We are not done exploring the ramifications of the work of Christ. First John 1:7 promises, "If we walk in the light, as he is in the light, we have fellowship with one another, and the blood of Jesus his Son cleanses us from all sin." Sin has a way of making us dirty. Think of a child going out after a rain and playing in the mud. That child's clothes are stained and filthy. They are ruined. Sin is like that. It stains. We need a deep-clean and fresh clothes. Then Jesus comes to earth and dies. His death has a power that washes us up and clothes us in pristine garments of righteousness.

Has sin's nastiness clung to you? Scripture teaches that God cleansed you at the cross. He washed away your spiritual grime. No religious rite or other sacrifice can replicate this.

> For if the blood of goats and bulls, and the sprinkling of defiled persons with the ashes of a heifer, sanctify for the purification of the flesh, how much more will the blood of Christ, who through the eternal Spirit offered himself without blemish to God, purify our conscience from dead works to serve the living God. (Hebrews 9:13–14)

You are pure before God because of what Jesus did.

Another way to describe this purity is *sanctification*. That is the word used in Hebrews 10:10. "We have been sanctified through the offering of the body of Jesus Christ once for all." This sanctification means you are set apart, holy, and perfected through Jesus's work on the cross. Even though you still struggle with sin, God also sees you in this moment through the lens of his perfect Son. "For by a single offering he has perfected for all time those who are being sanctified" (Hebrews 10:14). Sanctification has an already-and-not-yet reality to it. We are not perfect at this point, but God sees us outside of time as sanctified.

How many times have you failed, fallen, and fumbled? How many times have you tried not to go back and sin in the same way, yet you felt like you could not stop? God knows and saw it ahead of time. But when God looks at you in an eternal sense, he sees his Son. He doesn't see your sin. Jesus became the final offering for sin, transforming your moral rags to riches. I love how 2 Corinthians 5:21 puts it: "For our sake he made him to be sin who knew no sin, so that in him we might become the righteousness of God." You don't have a mere appearance of godliness; you have Christ's rightness through his finished work. You become the righteousness of God. This is not just wishful thinking.

This means you are *justified*, another technical word for "declared righteous and not guilty." This is a legal reality before a heavenly court. You are justified not based on anything you had done, but solely on what Jesus did. God superimposed Jesus's morality and purity on your history.

You are also reconciled. As far as God is concerned, if you truly trust in Christ as your Lord and Savior, he is good with you. Romans 5:10–11 says,

> If while we were enemies we were reconciled to God by the death of his Son, much more, now that we are reconciled, shall we be saved by his life. More than that, we also rejoice in God through our Lord Jesus Christ, through whom we have now received reconciliation. (see also Ephesians 2:16)

By faith, you no longer are estranged from your Creator. Your relationship is no longer awkward, uncomfortable, foreign, or dysfunctional. No, you are at peace with the King of kings and Lord of lords. He made you pure, clean, and just by the finished work of Christ.

God begins to change your heart. You begin to hate what he hates and love what he loves. Far too often, you and I get sucked into the cultural tide waters. Recognizing what Jesus did in dying for you, and understanding that he cleansed you and purified you, can help drive you to pursue godly choices in spite of cultural currents moving in the opposite direction.

Your cleansing was made real through Jesus. "It is finished."

THROUGH THE CROSS, WE ARE BROUGHT NEAR

This right standing results in an intimacy. Ephesians 2:13 says, "But now in Christ Jesus you who once were far off have been brought near by the blood of Christ." The sinful part of you and me would hide from God, but through Jesus's blood he comes near. He makes the first move. He jumps the fence. He runs to us. He bridged the distance that we made.

Hebrews 10:19 teaches, "We have confidence to enter the holy places by the blood of Jesus." If we ever met a president, or pope, or prime minister, I think we would naturally be a bit nervous. They tend to carry an air of authority and power. If we knew they had some scoop that we had broken one of their laws, our anxiety would sky rocket. Carry that analogy over to meeting God. We were lawbreakers, and he is the King of the universe. Meeting God should be a million times more disturbing.

However, Hebrews teaches that through Jesus's finished work at the cross, we can have the confidence to enter God's presence. We have no reason in ourselves to be so bold. Our courage exists because God overcame the gap and brings us near through the cross. God's grace and forgiveness and kindness have brought us close and given us backbone. What a gift. We can pray to

God without fear of reprisals. We can offer him our needs, worries, and dreams. We can tell him all. We can be honest. We can expose all of our deepest longings and disappointments and embarrassing sins. We don't need to cower before God or ignore what we really think and feel. When Jesus said, "It is finished," his death draws us near to God.

THROUGH THE CROSS, WE ARE DELIVERED

Beyond desiring to belong and be loved and be clean from sin, we also desire hope for the future. Galatians 1:4 tells us that Jesus "gave himself for our sins to deliver us from the present evil age, according to the will of our God and Father." Jesus's life delivers us from this evil age in a sense now and completely in the future. We may have to go through another difficult day, but not forever.

Romans 6:6 proclaims, "We know that our old self was crucified with him in order that the body of sin might be brought to nothing, so that we would no longer be enslaved to sin." You are free from the spiritual slavery of the past. Jesus crucified your old self at the cross. That self is dead and gone. Now you have new life from God that makes you able to resist sin and say no to the devil. Jesus has put your old self away. Will you?

That freedom also means that although Satan continues to tempt us, his reign of terror is terminal. Revelation 12:10–11 says,

> Now the salvation and the power and the kingdom of
> our God and the authority of his Christ have come, for
> the accuser of our brothers has been thrown down, who
> accuses them day and night before our God. And they
> have conquered him by the blood of the Lamb.

The accuser, our enemy, no longer has say over you. Hebrews 2:14 helps us understand Satan's doom further. "Since therefore

the children share in flesh and blood, he [Jesus] himself likewise
partook of the same things, that through death he might destroy
the one who has the power of death, that is, the devil." Genesis
3:15 prophesied this destruction, with its promise that the seed
of the woman would bruise the serpent's head. Jesus will destroy
the devil for good one day. No one, nothing can thwart that.
Jesus's finished work means Satan's days are numbered and his
power over you is not like it used to be.

We can have the confidence to fight sin like never before.
This is not arrogance or an inflated view of self. Substantively,
things have changed. Jesus altered the rules of engagement. He
died, defeating the curse that was before us. We can say no to sin
now. We need to fear the devil no longer. We can live our lives
with and for God because of what Jesus did on the cross. That is
what Jesus meant when he said, "It is finished."

THROUGH THE CROSS, WE HAVE A MISSION

How does it feel to be free from sin, loved, forgiven, and part of
something bigger than everything else? How does it feel to know
Jesus cares about you so much that he died? How does it feel to
be released from the destiny of this dark world and its evil grip?
It feels great, doesn't it? If we grasp what Jesus means, we can't
help but worship him.

Philippians 2:8–11 says of Jesus,

> And being found in human form, he humbled himself
> by becoming obedient to the point of death, even death
> on a cross. Therefore God has highly exalted him and
> bestowed on him the name that is above every name,
> so that at the name of Jesus every knee should bow, in
> heaven and on earth and under the earth, and every

tongue confess that Jesus Christ is Lord, to the glory of
God the Father.

While the devil is defeated, Jesus is exalted. We respond
in praise and honor. Indeed, the finished work of Christ is the
basis for song. If Jesus never died, we would have nothing to sing
about. We would be under the judgment of God, stuck in sin, and
bound to the powers of this world without God or hope.

Instead, Jesus's victory leads us on a mission. Knowing what
he has done and offers all who would believe propels us to gratitude, obedience, and witness. First Peter 2:24 puts it this way:
"He himself bore our sins in his body on the tree, that we might
die to sin and live to righteousness." Through Jesus's death, we
have a holy aim in life.

This aim allows us to unite with brothers and sisters, neighbors and strangers in new and exciting ways. Ephesians 2:14–15
says,

> For he himself is our peace, who has made us both one
> and has broken down in his flesh the dividing wall of
> hostility by abolishing the law of commandments
> expressed in ordinances, that he might create in himself
> one new man in place of the two, so making peace, and
> might reconcile us both to God in one body through the
> cross, thereby killing the hostility.

Caste systems and class distinctions don't need to divide us
in the church anymore. Our value before God is based not on
ancestry, race, gender, or age. We have a mission and aim, united,
at the cross. The cross broke down animosity between all of his
people. No room exists for sexism, racism, and or other similar
"isms" in light of the cross. Discrimination has no place in light

of Good Friday. Jesus destroyed all that through his death. What once separated people must not divide any longer. Our diversity represents God's creativity. We are stronger together than apart. The only reason we can be united as a church is through the finished work of Jesus. Jesus's finished work inspires worship and obedience. It propels us to move toward a relationship with others even when it is hard.

That unity expresses itself in a joint mission to make disciples of all nations. No people group is exempt from the Great Commission. Jesus's death moves us from being self-absorbed and hopeless to hope-filled, selfless lovers of people. We are given the assignment to reach our neighbors, co-workers, classmates, and family members with the truth of what Jesus finished on the cross. This is the type of mission we cannot go on alone. We need each other to reach all peoples. Jesus's finished work moves us to that end.

"It is finished."

REFLECTION

Jesus has done so much. It was all finished at the cross. Reflect on the totality of it now.

See Your Need. Take a spiritual inventory of your life and heart. How are you doing spiritually? What does your relationship with God look like? Where is your relationship with God coming up short?

See Jesus. As you read through all the finished work of the cross, which aspect stood out to you the most? Why do you think that was?

Come Near to God. Each section of this chapter points to a different ramification of Christ's finished work on the cross. How can you move toward Jesus because of what he has finished for you? (Perhaps you memorize a verse from the above passages, or list the ways you have sinned and God has forgiven you, or you plan a time to go on a personal retreat and draw near to God.)

Go to Others. In what way does the finished work of Christ free you to care for others? Whom do you know well enough to know they need to hear these truths? How might God use you to help one person understand one truth of about the finished work of Christ in the coming months?

Pray.

Thank you, Lord, for what was finished at the cross.
You are so merciful and loving. You do more on
the cross than I can comprehend. Open my eyes,
soften my heart, unplug my ears to make sense of
what happened two thousand years ago at Calvary.
Help that truth be a homing device for the lost to be
found, the sick to be healed, the hurting to be comforted, and a conduit communicating your grace.
Thank you for Good Friday.

7

Father

"Father, into your hands I commit my spirit!"
(Luke 23:46)

❧

We have arrived at the very last words of Christ on the cross. Luke records, "Then Jesus, calling out with a loud voice, said, 'Father, into your hands I commit my spirit!' And having said this he breathed his last" (Luke 23:46). This final saying was a prayer. Jesus ended as he began, talking to his Father. He committed his spirit to his Father's hands. What does that mean for us? What difference does what Jesus said make for our lives?

We recognize that Jesus was not talking to just any father or to his earthly stepfather, Joseph, but to God. We also recognize that when Jesus addressed God as Father, it meant more than it does when we call God our Father. There is a sense in which God, as our Creator who has adopted us as his children, is "Father of all" (Ephesians 4:6), and in the Lord's Prayer, Jesus himself taught us to call God our Father. However, Jesus's relationship to God was and is qualitatively different.

The Bible teaches that Jesus was and is the one and only Son of God (John 3:16). For eternity, he has been "in the form of God" (Philippians 2:6). In him, we see "all the fullness of God" (Colossians 1:19). He is perfectly God in his nature and glory, and his words carry all the authority of God, as the opening words of Hebrews explain when describing Jesus:

> Long ago, at many times and in many ways, God spoke to our fathers by the prophets, but in these last days he has spoken to us by his Son, whom he appointed the heir of all things, through whom also he created the world. He is the radiance of the glory of God and the exact imprint of his nature, and he upholds the universe by the word of his power. (Hebrews 1:1–3)

The angel Gabriel announced that Jesus was the "Son of the Most High" (Luke 1:32), as did John the Baptist (John 1:34). The disciples too called Jesus the Son of God (Matthew 14:33; John 1:49; 20:31), and Jesus spoke of himself as the Lord and Son of God (Matthew 7:21; Luke 22:29; John 5:17; 6:32; 8:54; 10:29; 14:23; 15:1). His enemies used this claim against him (Matthew 26:63; 27:40; Luke 22:70), as did the devil (Matthew 4:3). After Jesus ascended to heaven, his followers claimed again and again that he was the Son of God (Romans 1:4; 8:32; 1 Corinthians 1:9; Galatians 2:20; 4:6; Ephesians 4:13; Colossians 1:13).

Jesus's relationship with the Father is key to understanding the significance of Jesus's prayer. Jesus was not just a man; he was the God-man, the Son of God. His finished work on the cross was complete because he was not just fully man but fully God as well. Only a Savior who is God could live a perfectly sinless life required as our substitute. Only a Savior who is God could have the strength to endure the infinite wrath of God, and only a Savior who is God could be so infinitely valuable that his one sacrifice saves everyone who believes. His complete divinity and humanity give us confidence in his ability to save.

Jesus owned this identity. The earliest example we read of his self-awareness of who he was came at twelve. His family went to Jerusalem at Passover. When they left, most likely in a large caravan, Jesus remained behind unnoticed. He stayed in the temple with the teachers. He listened and questioned and answered them for three days.

When his parents finally returned and found him, I imagine they were quite shaken up. Jesus responded to them, "Why were you looking for me? Did you not know that I must be in my Father's house?" (Luke 2:49). I wonder how Joseph would have heard that? Joseph probably worked hard as a carpenter to support his family. He left everything he knew for a season to live in a foreign land protecting Jesus from King Herod (Matthew 2:13–14). In spite of all that, Jesus unapologetically was there in the temple talking about another Father while his parents were wondering about his safety. When they found him, his question might have felt downright rude.

While this may be, that was not necessarily Joseph's reaction. He understood something about Jesus's identity. He knew he was not Jesus's biological father. Years before, Joseph processed that fact when Mary was pregnant.

Did you catch what house Jesus referred to as his Father's house? He referred to the holy temple, God's special dwelling place in Jerusalem, not Joseph's home. Nazareth was not ultimately Jesus's home. It was Joseph's, but Jesus belonged to another place, God the Father's home. I think Joseph knew that. He and Mary understood Jesus was more than a good Israelite boy intently studying the Torah. Jesus had a unique relationship with God. He would carry his identity into his public ministry, regardless of the cost. He was and always would be the Son of God.

One of the most striking portrayals of Jesus's Sonship was in the garden of Gethsemane, hours before his death. There, Mark's account emphasizes Jesus's use of *Father* by recording not only the Greek word but also the Aramaic, *Abba*, used in everyday speech: "And he said, 'Abba, Father, all things are possible for you. Remove this cup from me. Yet not what I will, but what you will'" (Mark 14:36). At that time Jesus was suffering so much so that his sweat was like drops of blood. Jesus was anticipating his imminent death on the cross as he plead to God his Father.

In Jesus's final gasps of life, hours later, we see this same intimacy. He had an affection for God. The rest of Scripture indicates that unique love went both ways. Matthew records a voice from heaven announcing, "This is my beloved Son, with whom I am well pleased" (Matthew 3:17). The Father loves the Son, and the Son loves the Father. God was pleased with Jesus. Twice God spoke like this, once at his baptism and again at the transfiguration (Matthew 17:5).

OUR FATHER TOO

Jesus's Sonship not only reminds us of his unique saving power and identity, but also reminds us of our adoption into God's family. First John 3:1 states, "See what kind of love the Father has given to us, that we should be called children of God; and so we are." By love, through the finished work of Christ on the cross, God adopts us as his own. We too have him for a Father. John writes, "But to all who did receive him, who believed in his name, he gave the right to become children of God, who were born, not of blood nor of the will of the flesh nor of the will of man, but of God" (John 1:12–13). Through faith, by grace we are born again in the power of the Holy Spirit by Jesus's death on the cross. God truly adopts those who truly believe into his family forever.

This adoption is incredible! J. I. Packer writes, "Adoption . . . is the highest privilege that the gospel offers."* *Gospel* means "good news." The greatest news on the whole planet is that we become children of God. God supersedes blood bonds, bringing you and me into his family. This adoption is not contingent on us, but on God's gracious and merciful work in our hearts bringing about faith and transformation (Ephesians 2:8–9). We become sons and daughters of the King of the universe, the Creator of everything, the Lord of all. This adoption is more than an affiliation. Paul writes,

> For all who are led by the Spirit of God are sons of God. For you did not receive the spirit of slavery to fall back into fear, but you have received the Spirit of adoption as sons, by whom we cry, "Abba! Father!" The Spirit himself bears witness with our spirit that we are children of God. (Romans 8:14–16; see also Galatians 4:4–7)

Through the Holy Spirit, we can humbly join Jesus in appealing to God intimately as *Abba, Father.* That is radical! How can we call God this ancient form of "Dad"? It seems so brazen and audacious. Jesus paved the way for our appeal by dying on our behalf. This adoption is part of what resulted in his finished work that day.

We belong to the Father by faith. We are his! We have been adopted into the family of God. "But when the fullness of time had come, God sent forth his Son, born of woman, born under the law, to redeem those who were under the law, so that we might receive adoption as sons" (Galatians 4:4–5). Is this comforting to you? Does it feel like the highest privilege, as J. I. Packer asserts? Maybe you recoil at the thought as God as your Father because

* J. I. Packer, *Knowing God* (Downers Grove, IL: InterVarsity, 1973), 186.

of your past experience. Don't let a bad earthly father distort the heavenly one. Regardless of your parents, by grace through faith, you can experience a relationship no parent could ever offer. No one is like our God. The heavenly Father won't yell at you to get his way. He won't neglect you because he is too busy with work. He won't be rude, abusive, or mean. He was and is and always will be loving, patient, gracious, merciful, and kind. If you want to know how much he loves you, consider how he willingly exchanged his one and only Son for you to be adopted forever.

The very last thing Jesus said was an offering of himself to his loving Father. Why? I think categorically Jesus understands his Father's nature. God is love. God is good. God is kind and compassionate. He is slow to anger, merciful, and gracious. Through Jesus's death, this very same God is our Father too by faith!

God's care for us is personal and kind. We too can submit our lives to his hands like Jesus did. We can trust him. He is not a distant force pulling some strings. The fatherhood of God means you can have confidence to talk with and listen to him in any moment of the day. You have access to him in a way those who don't believe can't. The access a president's son or daughter has is completely different than a stranger. That child's access is the kind of access you have to God, but better. In difficult circumstances you can experience his personal ministry and discipline. He protects you from yourself in visible and invisible ways. In love he sends his Spirit to convict you of sin and puts the brakes on destructive behaviors through the conscience and outside forces. At times he brings Scripture to mind to curb your disobedience, or he sends distractions. Have you experienced that? That is an expression of the Father's care for you, his child.

Not only does the fatherhood of God result in an intimate relationship with you, but he has a wonderful inheritance in store for you in heaven. What Jesus said in the upper room hours before his death applies to all of God's adopted children:

"Let not your hearts be troubled. Believe in God; believe also in me. In my Father's house are many rooms. If it were not so, would I have told you that I go to prepare a place for you? And if I go and prepare a place for you, I will come again and will take you to myself, that where I am you may be also." (John 14:1–3)

Death did not destroy Jesus. He willingly embraced death to bring us a heavenly home. That home is one where there is no sickness, no sadness, no sorrow, no tears, no pain, and no sin (Revelation 21:1–4). Instead, there is joy unending. God has riches beyond all measure for you his child. Peter described our unbelievable inheritance as "imperishable, undefiled, and unfading, kept in heaven for you" (1 Peter 1:4). The inventor of everything you and I enjoy—everything—promises an inheritance far better than anything we could ever ask for or imagine (Ephesians 3:20). The greatest treasure of all is the Father himself. He is greater than all things conceived and combined. Heaven is going to be amazing. You and I have an unmatched inheritance because of this adoption.

This adoptive reality can mitigate fear. Often we worry about the future. *Whom will I marry, where will I go to school, and what should I study? Where should I work? What home should I buy? How will we educate our kids? How can I live on this income? What is going to happen in the future?* The worries of the future can flood our minds in a moment. Through Jesus's example and work, we can grasp that we have a loving Father on our side. We don't have to worry. He has the ultimate best in mind for us. As rough as things might turn out for us, we can commit ourselves to the Father's hands like Jesus did. That is comforting.

Another comforting truth flowing from the fatherhood of God is that the relationship is irrevocable. God won't change his mind. Once adopted, he doesn't disown. If you truly believe, then your relationship to God is secure. He won't turn his back on you. The reason we know this is because of the testimony of Scripture. Jesus, himself, said in John 10.

> "My sheep hear my voice, and I know them, and they follow me. I give them eternal life, and they will never perish, and no one will snatch them out of my hand. My Father, who has given them to me, is greater than all, and no one is able to snatch them out of the Father's hand. I and the Father are one." (John 10:27–30)

No one will snatch you out of the Father's hand. You can trust your Father. You can put your life in his hands. He has got you.

Jesus wasn't anxious in his final breaths, nor do we need to be. Jesus knew who he was and where he was going. He knew who his Father was and could trust him completely. He could commit himself to his Father. Through our adoption, we too have God as our Father. We don't need to fret. God is faithful. He is trustworthy. He is strong. We can rest assure our adoption is signed and sealed by the blood of Christ. We can trust in God the Father.

LIFE WITH GOD AS FATHER

If adoption is true, then what? If God is your Father, then when you begin to feel guilt, instead of trying to numb the sense with busyness or noise, you can stop and listen to your Father. God is likely speaking to you through the Spirit in those thoughts helping you probe your heart. Slow down. Ask, *Why am I feeling this sense of guilt? Is there a command I violated?* For example, you could ask, *Was my action loving, patient, kind, gentle, or self-controlled? Were my actions worldly or Spirit-led* (Galatians 5:22–25)? *Was I quick to listen, slow to speak, slow to become angry* (James 1:19)? Allow God to speak to you about your sin and remind you of his loving provision in Jesus's death for that sin.

If God is your Father, consider your circumstances. God as Father directs your steps. Maybe the Father is disciplining you when things don't go your way. Possibly God is blocking you from a path of danger. Perhaps he is leading you to a greener pasture. God is sovereign and good. He loves his children. Thank him for protecting you and guiding you with his hands in your circumstances. You never know what hardships and darkness may have been your reality had the Father left you alone.

If God is your Father, he hears you. Have you ever thought, "Does God even hear my prayers?" I think we all have wrestled with some doubts from time to time. As a child of God, we can bank on the promises of Scripture that the Father hears his children. He is not deaf to your cries. He knows your pain and suffering. He is fully aware. He listens. He cares. The Father hears you.

If God is your Father, be comforted in your future inheritance. This inheritance is unlike anything you could ever amass or imagine. The Bible says God has written eternity on mankind's heart (Ecclesiastes 3:11). You and I long for something beyond us. I believe ultimately that yearning is for God, himself. The heartache of loneliness or homesickness are echoes of our need for the Father and subsequent blessings. If you have ever had a desire for Camelot or Eden, that longing will soon be fulfilled as children of God. Time is short. Soon you will find ourselves before the Creator of everything. At that time, those of us who call him Father through Jesus's finished work will see firsthand that we were made to dwell with him all along. It will be better than anything you have ever dreamed (1 Corinthians 2:9). You can pass through the trials in life, being comforted in the future inheritance found in your adoption into God's family.

REFLECTION

These realities are only possible through Jesus, the Son of God's death on your behalf. The Fatherhood of God is extended to you through what Jesus did and reverberates in his committing himself into the Father's hands. That is astounding. Reflect on what this means:

See Your Need. Describe a time where you felt God was distant, not like a loving Father. Was there a point where you felt like your prayers were falling on deaf ears or his hand was heavy upon you? Was there a time you felt alone or lost in life?

See Jesus. Envision Jesus's final breaths. He commits himself to his heavenly Father's hands. He shares that intimacy with you by dying on your behalf. His Father becomes your Father as well through faith in Jesus's death on your behalf. When you think of being his child, what do you long for most, right now? (Do you want relief from the tyranny of trials? Are you looking for your prayers to be heard? Do you want to see the Father's guidance? Are you yearning for fatherly comfort?)

Come Near to God. What are your prayers like these days? Do you talk to God as Father like Jesus does? How can you explore the Father's strong loving care for you, his child this week? (Perhaps you journal all the ways you see God's care, or maybe you attend a study on God's love and strength, or maybe you explore what hymns talk about God's love.) How might you move toward interacting with God as your Father more?

Go to Others. Understanding the nature of God as Father, how might that impact how you care for those around you in the coming weeks? For example, since God is a loving Father, how might you express God's love to others? Possibly the most challenging people to care for are those closest to you (spouse, child, parent, or someone you work with). Write a goal to express the Father's love to someone. Dream about what might happen if you commit your life into his hands. Make a step toward that goal. Put it down on a to-do list, and see God work.

Pray.

Heavenly Father, thank you for sending your one and only Son to die in my place. Thank you for giving me faith in your Son. Thank you for making a way for me to call you Father through faith. I have not had a perfect experience growing up, but you are perfect. I know I have fallen short of your perfection myself. God help me to demonstrate how great you are to the watching world and comfort my weak soul as I journey through life. I love you, Father. I commit my heart, mind, body, and soul to you. Thank you for Good Friday.

Epilogue

~

Do you like extra credit? In school, I was always doing extra credit. Here is a bonus chapter and challenge for you. How do you sum up all of Jesus's last words on the cross? Does that seem possible?

Do you carry your sin like a tattoo on your forehead and need Jesus's word of forgiveness to erase it? Do you want a hope beyond this life and find Jesus's word to the thief an encouragement? Do you long for someone to offer you a little compassion in your trials, so that you find Jesus's word to his mother and disciple comforting? Is your heart filled with worship as you comprehend the extraordinary exchange that took place as Jesus was forsaken? Does Jesus's humanity as seen in his thirst speak to your desire to be understood? Does Jesus's finished work on the cross amaze you and leave you speechless? Does Jesus's divinity and our intimacy with God the Father bring you joy and relief? How do you respond to the last words of Christ on the cross?

Microscopes magnify what is small yet close, and telescopes magnify what is far yet big. They both help us see in new ways.

Art is similar. It can bring spiritual things into view and put ideas into perspective. Painting, drawing, sculpture, photography, and poetry are examples of ways to express oneself and creatively explore the world. Meter and rhyme and cadence can focus one's eye and ear and heart. Poetic rules can push the mind and strengthen understanding. To answer my question, "How do you sum up all of Jesus's last words in your own words?" I summarized what happened to Jesus on the cross in poetic form.

I don't claim to be a poet. However, this exercise was worshipful for me. Maybe it will be for you as you read it. I hope this poem will provide kindling to prompt you to explore your creativity, help you see what Jesus did through fresh eyes, and worship in new and wonderful ways.

THIS WAS GOOD FRIDAY

Amidst the day the sky went black
Light from the sun would not come back
At least this hour, this day, for now
The mourners left their shoulders bowed
This was Good Friday

The dead were raised and curtain torn
A mother and her new son mourn
A mocking crowd, religious jeer
A criminal forgiven here
This was Good Friday

Christ had cried out to his Father
"Dad, here is my life I offer
I give up my life and my ghost
Abba is whom I long for most"
This was Good Friday

Breathing my last I die today
On this planet I will not stay
Exalted now with God on high
Followers wait and wonder why
This was Good Friday

It started before time began
The glory of a Triune plan
Earth, water, sky, sun, moon, and star
Soon everything made near and far

Complete the creation now is known
Man out of dust and woman bone
Designer's perfect very good
Innocent and pleasing they stood

Satan, morning star, Lucifer
Devil, deceiver, accuser
Serpent, dragon, angel of light
Had hopes of evil to incite

This crafty fallen archangel
His pride being instrumental
Presents lies to Eve, God's woman
First, she falls for it, then the man

Shock and knowledge of good and bad
Shame, sorrow of what they once had
Innocence gone and friendship lost
A simple bite at Eden's cost

This all Christ saw years long ago
The pain of rebellion he knows
A curse was said by God himself
Seed of woman will be her help

This snake would first bruise his heel
The woman's seed would crush the deal
And bring comfort to the sour
Predicting a future hour

As a young man, I worked the saw
And studied the Creator's law
Then was baptized by my cousin
Found some disciples: a dozen

I took them to a wedding feast
I turned water and wine increased
I fed thousands and healed the sick
Cast out demons; this was no trick

I taught by power; raised the dead
Challenged systems; and turned some heads
Walked on water and calmed the storm
Satisfied prophecies to form

My perfect life upsets leaders
A prophet, priest, and king appears
Pointing hearts to the true God
Pharisees seek out a death squad

In that holy land of promise
City of Zion; my office
On the week of that Passover
I gave my life; kept composure
This was Good Friday

Betrayed, and spat on, beat, and bruised
Lied to, insulted, and abused
I suffered for the world's sin
Embracing God's just wrath for them
This was Good Friday

"Father forgive them," was my plea
Not knowing whom they hung on tree
They did not know I made the nail
Did not know God's plan would not fail
This was Good Friday

A criminal joined the mockers
Pain through body as the gawkers
Called for miracles from on high
Not believing any are nigh
This was Good Friday

Yet another thief will believe
He will rebuke and trust in me
I will offer a hope for him
Place in paradise, free from sin
This was Good Friday

My good friend became a child
Will aid mother in a while
My torture now is so extreme
I see my Father far from me
This was Good Friday

Suffering all your wrath for sin
Bearing guilt of world within
I am divided and punished
Redemption would be accomplished
This was Good Friday

Thirsting now my task is complete
Humankind and the divine meet
Fulfilling ancient prophecy
I take a drink for all to see
This was Good Friday

"It is finished," I proclaimed
God's work complete I take the blame
All your guilt and sin on myself
By faith in me, you find your health
This was Good Friday

These the last words that I do say,
"Into your hands," on this sad day
"I commit my spirit," spoken
Not one of my bones were broken
This was Good Friday

The darkness that envelops me
It gives you all your liberty
Forgiven, purified, and loved
I am more than all you've dreamed of
This was Good Friday

So weep and mourn, give up your sin
Reverse your course, let me break in
Allow my Spirit to have say
And receive my love in this way
This was Good Friday

Jesus was in total control as he died. He gave up his spirit willingly. It was not taken from him. He knew his destination. He was going to his Father.

Jesus was and is infinite, mysterious, and magnificent. He was and is God. God is higher, greater, and superlative to all. Take a moment to explore your own creativity. There's space to do it right here. You may be surprised at what you discover.

Pray.

Jesus, I commit my life to you. Thank you for giving
your life for me. Your words show me who you are
and what you are about. Thank you for being forgiving, loving, considerate, selfless, humble, powerful, and true. I accept your forgiveness and commit
myself to you. Help me to follow you, love you, and
know you more and more. Fill my heart with gratitude and worship for your glory. May my worship
spill over to grateful service to those around the
rest of my days. Thank you for Good Friday.

Bibliography

Alleine, Joseph. *The Precious Promises of the Gospel.* Orlando, FL: Soli Deo Gloria, 2000.

Anderson-Berry, David. *The Seven Sayings of Christ on the Cross.* Glasgow: Pickering & Inglis, 1920.

Balthasar, Hans Urs von. *Mysterium Paschale: The Mystery of Easter.* San Francisco: Ignatius Press, 2005.

Chandler, Matt. *Explicit Gospel.* Wheaton IL: Crossway, 2014.

Edwards, W. D. "On the Physical Death of Jesus Christ." *JAMA: The Journal of the American Medical Association* 255, no. 11 (March 21, 1986): 1455–1463. doi:10.1001/jama.255.11.1455.

Gilbert, Greg. *What Is the Gospel?* Wheaton, IL: Crossway, 2010.

Grudem, Wayne. *Bible Doctrine.* Grand Rapids, MI: Zondervan, 2015.

Grudem, Wayne A., and K. Erik Thoennes. *Systematic Theology.* Grand Rapids, MI: Zondervan, 2008.

Hauerwas, Stanley. *Cross-Shattered Christ: Meditations on the Seven Last Words.* Grand Rapids, MI: Brazos Press, 2004.

Lewis, C. S. *The Lion, the Witch, and the Wardrobe.* Waterville, ME: Thorndike Press, 2017.

Lloyd-Jones, Sally. *The Jesus Storybook Bible: Every Story Whispers His Name.* Grand Rapids, MI: Zonderkidz, 2014.

Lucado, Max. *No Wonder They Call Him Savior: Discover Hope in the Unlikeliest Place.* Sisters, OR: Multnomah, 1985.

Mahaney, C. J. *The Cross Centered Life.* Sisters, OR: Multnomah, 2002.

McDowell, Josh, and Sean McDowell. *More Than a Carpenter.* Wheaton, IL: Tyndale House, 2011.

Neuhaus, Richard John. *Death on a Friday Afternoon: Meditations on the Last Words of Jesus From the Cross.* New York: Basic Books, 2000.

O'Reilly, Bill, and Martin Dugard. *Killing Jesus.* New York: Henry Holt, 2013.

Packer, J. I. *Knowing God.* London: Hodder & Stoughton, 2013.

Pink, A. W. *The Seven Sayings of the Saviour on the Cross.* Grand Rapids, MI: Baker, 1984.

Piper, John. *Seeing and Savoring Jesus Christ: Study Guide Developed by Desiring God.* Wheaton, IL: Crossway, 2008.

Piper, John. *50 Reasons Why Jesus Came to Die.* Wheaton, IL: Crossway, 2006.

Poirier, Dr. Alfred J. "The Cross and Criticism." *The Journal of Biblical Counseling* 17, no. 3 (Spring 1999).

peacemaker-ministries.mybigcommerce.com/content/The%20 Cross%20and%20Criticism.pdf.

Seitz, Christopher R. *Seven Lasting Words: Jesus Speaks from the Cross.* Louisville, KY: Westminster John Knox Press, 2001.

Stott, John R. W. *The Cross of Christ.* Downers Grove, IL: InterVarsity, 2006.

Strobel, Lee. *Case for Christ.* Grand Rapids, MI: Zondervan, 2016.

Vincent, Milton. *A Gospel Primer: for Christians.* Bemidji, MN: Focus Publishing, 2008.

Index of Scripture